A Love of Our Own

Passion, Purpose, and Poetry

K. Antwon Buckner

CLF Publishing, LLC.
9161 Sierra Ave, Ste. 203C
Fontana, CA 92335
www.clfpublishing.org

Cover Design by Senir Design. Contact information-info@senirdesign.com.

ISBN # 978-1-945102-05-9

Printed in the United States of America.

Acknowledgments

First and foremost, to my creator Jehovah: Thank you for the gift of life, and the many blessings: deserving and the blessings I didn't deserve but was given through grace.

To my mother: Your push, strength, and courage inspired me to grow beyond my beliefs. Your love has always given me comfort, and your words keep me reminded that with faith and works, I can move mountains. Thank you.

To my Pops: Thanks for the many lessons and teachings on how to be a man when I was coming of age. Good lookin', Pops!

To my sisters: Words can't describe the depths of my love. Thank you for standing by me, right and wrong. Constantly, I remain.

To my dear friend and mentor, Stephen (Romeo) Williams: You inspired me beyond words. You have a great mind, and your advice was not unheard. Thanks, Bro.

To all who have given me true friendship without waiver, thank you. I'm grateful to the people in my life who supported me while dealing with the depths of my lows, encouraging me, many times unknowingly, to achieve the highs of success.

SHMACK SHMACK! Last, but not least, to Gabriela Plascencia: You came into my life at the perfect time. You are amazing. And, the love is real.

Passionately, I remain.

Statement of Gratitude

One can only be extremely grateful to all who have chosen to partake in this long journey. May this book be embraced with an open mind while understanding its purpose is to build. Your time, interest, and support are valued. This is more than words - this is an answer to questions many of us have. It is a sense of insight of the state of mind concerning love, relationships, trust, passion, and purpose in this era in which we live. My only hope is that one perhaps grasps something positive or inspiring from the reading.

It's incumbent upon us as humans to love and be loved by others and ourselves to obtain success in our lives. While embracing our passions and defining our purpose in life, let's turn our potential into performance-creating landmarks, not only establishing, but leaving beautiful and positive impacts that will reflect our legacy.

Table of Contents

SYNOPSIS
(Introduction)

A Love of Our Own was inspired by millions of people who search for love and a purpose, just as myself.

I understand it can be frustrating and also detrimental at times. So, I felt compelled to engage in this matter, in hopes of inspiring or perhaps sparking a bit, if not a lot, of motivation. I believe there is a message in the writing.

Love of our own is love itself, love of our companionship, and love of life, along with having love for our passions, while honing that passion, as we recognize and embrace our purpose.

We all have a purpose of passions in this lifetime, with a desire to find a love we can appreciate.

It's natural to desire to obtain a companion's love. It is a reflection of what we give.

In regards to equality, loyalty and reciprocity in every form, many search until they find a reflection of their love.

So, to be blessed with a platform, I thought, *What better way to share with the masses in regards to love, passion and purpose?*

Poetry happens to be a passion of mine, so in closing, I shared my passion for that.

I discovered a love of my own (in companionship and purpose): pursuing my passion.

It's my hope that each and every person breathing finds that love, passion and purpose and achieves......

Stay wide-eyed and alert for my poetry book *Kindred Souls*.

K. Antwon Buckner

PART ONE

Love and Passion

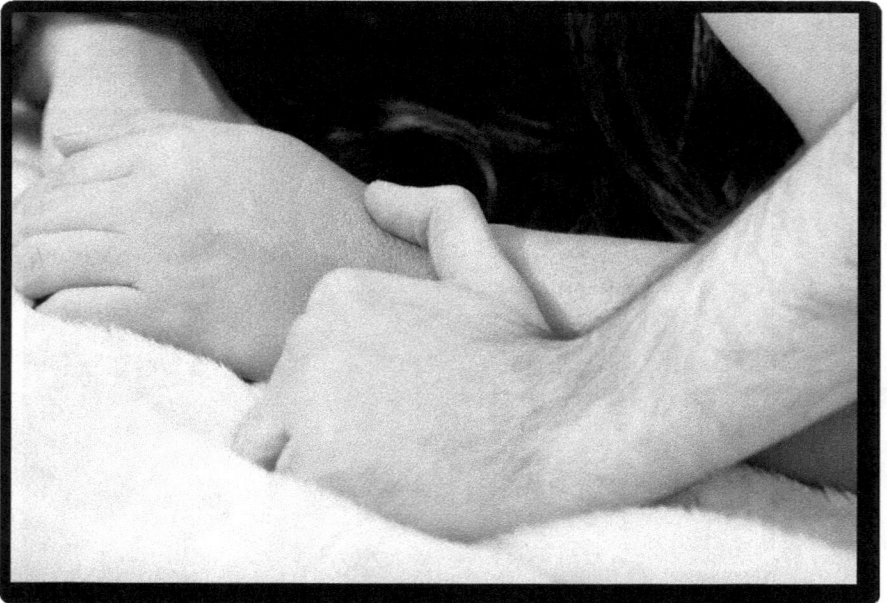

The simplicity of love and passion in this new era of technology and hook-ups can be complex but only when handled in an untruthful manner. Most of us human beings have a strong desire to be passionately loved, with our minds captivated and hearts conquered, while being swept off our feet, physically and mentally being enraptured whole-heartedly, considering every word to be poetic and every deed in truth. I have come to realize that love is an action. It is a behavior. It is also attitude and thoughts. Love is accepting one's likes and dislikes. Love is patient and unwavering.

I am sure all would agree that love should always come with reciprocity. For instance, no person likes to be the only one giving. In any affair, there should always be equality, and it should be genuine in all aspects. For example, if I should come home from taking care of business or a basic day at work to find dinner made or a nice hot bath waiting for me, without me asking, I am inclined to take heed to those lovely gestures. These are considered basic forms of love and affection. Naturally, I am inclined, genuinely and effortlessly, to respond to these acts in similar forms, out of love, respect and acknowledgement, thereby, establishing reciprocity, as the love that I speak of does not want. All that is desired is given without fault and is a true unconditional love in every sense, regardless of the opinions of others or the change of another's feelings. This love I speak of is an all enduring, true love. But to understand and embrace this kind of love, we must first come to truly love ourselves. (This will be discussed in depth later.)

However, some people (whom I find regularly) think love only comes in time. In fact, they could not be further from the truth. Any human being is capable of loving or being loved in a year, a month or a day. The simple truth is we are emotional creatures and a connection can be established at any given moment. Dealing with high levels of energy, good chemistry, intensity, and a strong mental connection can plant a seed for love. Case in point: I have always heard the term, "Love is blind."

Now, I never understood the meaning of this saying until I was succumbing to it. There I was interested in establishing a relationship with a close and personal friend. (May I point out that we had been friends for a little over two years at that time?) Furthermore, while appreciating the kindness, loyalty, and confidence shared between the two of us, I began to develop a deeper feeling of passion and connection that had evolved into love. Even though I had not planned to feel that way, I had to completely express myself.

So, I built up the courage and shared my feelings, stating how I desired more than a friendship and that I had developed feelings of love. Now, at that point, it seemed as though the whole world had stopped as I anticipated a response! And finally the words came, "Sorry, I don't feel the same way on that level." Honestly, I was stuck for a moment. And then and only then, I started to consider the coined phrase, "Love is blind." I learned how powerful and uncontrollable love is. I had established a love I was not seeking, did not see coming, and yet was in it alone. And at that moment, in a sense, love was blind. However, I am proud to say we still remain friends to this day and share an amazing bond as one shared by siblings. But all was created through energy, chemistry, and an intense mental connection.

Now, take a moment and think about love and fear. It is impossible to love when living with fear of the past or even what might be. Fear has no place in love. True, many of us have had our share of heartbreaks or bad-ending love affairs. However, we must consider each relationship as its own journey and treat each love uniquely, in its own way.

I take pleasure, as we all should, in embracing love and not letting fear control me. It takes courage to love, to put yourself out there. We must never let fear keep us from succeeding. Love is always worth taking a chance. In all my years of seeking love and knowing people that I have loved, I have learned a few things. I believe it is universal when I say we all look for honesty, loyalty, sincerity and security.

Let us take honesty for example. Honesty can be a two-edged sword. We all require this trait in our mate though we sometimes find it hard to deal with when dealt to us about something hurtful. Yet, how can we love without honesty? I mean, let us be serious. I am reluctant to create any form of relationship, friendship, love affair, etc. if I am not sure it is honest. Without the certainty of honesty, I place myself at greater risk of being the victim of lies, deceit, and ups and downs of an emotional tailspin. And nobody desires to deal with love for the fun of it, to have our emotions extracted from us due to measures of dishonesty. But a love that is created and established with honesty is a love that endures and withstands time and adversity.

Most couples think adversity builds character. I have come to learn by experience that adversity merely reveals the truth of one's character. Even the truest of loves are tested, measured and weighed. But honest love relationships prevail. Here is where I may lose you. Security and loyalty go hand in hand. When dealing with love, we all look for a loyal mate and one who can provide security. These qualities can be found in a confident person. Every time I search out a person, I look for confidence. Because then and only then will I be able to escape the ugliness of jealousy, which is not becoming in a mate. Jealousy brings destruction into the fold, thereby creating insecurity and planting a seed for disloyalty. We should all not only seek loyalty but demand it. Because not only does it ensure that we have a partner we can trust, but it provides a strong bond and security that is needed in a relationship.

Honestly speaking, there is nothing more rewarding in love than to feel secure with a loyal person. It pains me deeply that it is getting harder to find love, loyalty, security and commitment, especially because we now live in a new age called the hook-up era. And for many who do not understand or are unfamiliar with the term or lifestyle, allow me to elaborate. It is a disconnection of the very core principles of love. There is no mental captivation or any form of security or getting to know and understand the other person. One does not even consider a relationship. It is relations without a connection, emotional component, or time investment. Believe it or not, this lifestyle is counterproductive to bonding. It becomes a habit and eventually disassociates one from his/her emotional side.

Now, I am not going to say I have not subscribed to this term or lifestyle before, because I would be untruthful. I have, and what I can say is it was not conducive to me or the lifestyle I desire. Anyone can hook up or have relations. But it takes a human being to display love and affection, to demonstrate an open mind and heart for romance, and to have the ability to create a deep connection of passion and love.

Note: Just a month ago, a few friends and I had a small gathering. You know, nothing major, just reuniting: three male friends and myself and four female friends. Now, this very same topic came up, about the hook-up era. So, we all talked and exchanged our dispositions on the topic. Surprisingly, the women in our group defended the term. And the guys suggested that they would appeal to love and relationship rather than a basic hook-up.

Yes, I know, it is surprising. However, in defense of my female friends' answers, there were various reasons that were given for being favorable to the hook-up. First, the hook-up is conducive to attending school and work and when one does not have the time to become fully involved. The women stated their careers came first. So, there we all were debating about the subject of love and commitment versus the hook-up. My conclusion was that this was a subjective topic because you cannot tell a person that his/her education or career is not important, if in fact that is the reason for indulging in brief hook-ups and not wanting commitment. However, I did add any great thing worth attaining takes sacrifice. Growing up in a household with a mother and two sisters, I have gained a profound respect and love for women as the beauty of this universe, and they are worth taking the time to establish a relationship.

Furthermore, as a man, I believe men are the protectors of women, and women provide a strong source of mental strength for us. I speak to all men when I say we should appreciate and love all women. And women should support men and confirm our position in their life. Love is equal. Men do not serve women, and women do not serve men.

We confidently strive for achievement together, demonstrating security, honor, loyalty, kindness, tolerance, understanding, passion, support, truth and love, remaining true to form for the duration. Now, this is just my opinion and views of love. And of course this thing called love can be a subject we discuss. But, I believe it is only one authentic love that I embrace.

I have met some wonderful women in life, and I have been in love a few times. I loved in different ways and on different levels. I have fallen deeply in love, but never have I stayed. Only because once in love and my mate feels secure, things start to break down. I tend to notice a change in attitude, behavior and sometimes affection. And that always becomes a breaking point for me. Maybe I am unique, but I need to be loved with great energy. And I need all of me captivated, meaning physically, mentally and emotionally. We are physical beings, sexually affectionate and passionate. In love, these traits must be present in conquering one's heart.

Now, mentally a woman has to be able to captivate a man's mind. Mental stimulation is vital to any relationship/love. It keeps one considering each day a challenge, always learning something new. Just when I think I have figured my mate out, body language included, she throws a curve ball, and I learn something new. It is mental. I am not saying that women have to be scholars. I am only saying that men like a mental challenge. A form of intellect maintains the captivation indeed. Truly, the grown women can feel me.

So that is physically and mentally, and now for the third aspect: emotionally. Regardless of how strong the physical is or how great the mental has been, an emotional connection has to be established for a complete and full passage to falling in love. Some may think this only refers to considering one's feelings by supporting them when they are feeling down or expressing love. But the emotional aspect I speak of involves communication. Dialogue is very important in every love relationship and in any companionship. We must communicate on all levels and about all things. There must be no secrets, but full openness, from our strongest dreams and desires to the very things that we both dislike.

These forms of comfortable communication methods are great at keeping hopes and reality in perspective and respecting the boundaries of each other's likes and dislikes. To keep things bottled up is never good and is not a form of love. That is why I find the following three elements required in true love: physical, mental and emotional. And no, they do not have to be obtained in that order; however, each one must be present. So, all my ladies and all my dudes, love is a wonderful thing, so do not be such a critic of it. Instead, give it a chance. You might just like the journey.

As we move on, allow me to share a tip for men that is also good for women. Here are a few approaches I found in my favor when directed towards my lady. And I believe they will assist any man in any relationship. So, check me out fellas.

Note to serous couples- This requires sincerity because women know when a guy is gaming or being honest. If living together, when you wake up next to your woman, start the day off right. Take a few minutes to exchange a few kisses and love while gently caressing her. Communicate for a few seconds about what your plans are for the day. Show a little concern before the two of you separate for the day. Upon separating, tell her that you love her and you wish for her to have a beautiful day. Such attention will please her. And note: Every night when you go to sleep, never go to bed upset. And, always engage her in conversation. See how her day went and appeal to her. Eye contact is important. Show concern for nothing else but you and her. So that means no ESPN. All acknowledgements are towards her. Show some affection! Caress and cuddle- all that. Make sure she knows it is all about her. These are just some bonding steps that will create good energy and vibes.

Love and Commitment

Why do words like commitment, relationship, dedication, exclusivity, etc. scare some people? As if these were some types of diseases or plagues. First off, I do not consider myself a love guru or a lecturer. But, I do enjoy expressing myself on many topics. I assure you I do not prohibit myself from writing things that are real to me, or something I can relate to, such as commitment and relationships. To be in a relationship means you are committed, and honestly, commitment is one of the hardest things in a relationship to obtain, especially when the world offers irresistible options, such as 'temptation and lust' and 'revenge and distrust.' These can be considered four of the main factors in violating the code of commitment.

If I must say, revenge and distrust can be two of the ugliest things ever to be brought into a relationship. Maybe it is just me, but I believe it is almost human nature to seek revenge. A lot of us may not want to admit it, but we are a retaliatory species, which was instilled in us during our childhood, starting on the school playground. That is another topic of debate in itself, however.

When in relationships, we may often find ourselves in a position seeking revenge strictly for something that was done to us in the relationship. Maybe it was physical harm, or maybe it was mental harm, or possibly the other person's actions, either what they were doing or what they were not doing. Could it be something we saw and did not ask about that was just misread?

Whatever the case may be, these tend to be some of the contributing factors in revenge when involved in a committed relationship. So, let us be honest, as we are done identifying some of the contributing and controlling factors. Let us see if we can extract a solution to alleviate revenge from being a destructive component in any committed relationship. First off, if any male or female is being physically or mentally abused in any situation- leave, bounce, shake, remove yourself. All the above. That is not a relationship- period. Regardless of how good the sex is or how great the apology is after the abuse, you are in not in a relationship.

Now, obviously it is something your mate is doing to you, which he/she is not aware of that is driving the wedge between you two. Or possibly some attention is not being shown, or something that he/she is or is not doing that is making you act in a revengeful or distrustful way, such as stepping out of the relationship and being uncommitted in some form or fashion (mentally, physically, or emotionally). The simple answer to fixing the problem is Relationship 101. Communication is key.

Please do not underestimate dialogue. Instead of acting on these issues, bring them to light. No matter how big or how small the issue is, talk about it. Discuss what is happening that needs to stop. Also bring up what is not happening that needs to be. You should never be ashamed, bashful or afraid to discuss anything with your partner. When you cannot talk freely and speak your mind, minor issues become bottled up and they fester, turning into resentment and distrust, creating the setting for revenge and strife, which is counterproductive to you and your committed relationship. Therefore, express yourself always.

One final thing in keeping the ugly face of revenge or distrust from arising in the commitment is to never assume! We as humans always tend to assume or misread things. So, I say simply, "Don't!" It is unhealthy by far.

Another point I would like to raise is in regards to temptation and lust. Giving in to the seduction of appearances and lustful behavior is hard to refrain from. We become tempted sometimes at the very thought of beauty. And that temptation draws us into a lustful mindset. I am sure we all love beauty and are attracted to physical appearances and kind words.

Primarily, flirtatious body language is indeed tempting. I must honestly say, in our minds, we desire to be honest in our relationship, but our tempting nature can be hard to overcome. I heard it all, "Stay focused," "Ignore compliments," "Decline attention," anything you can think of. Surely, it is easier said than done. Once put in that situation, only then can you feel the pressure of true temptation. Now, the fact that temptation arises in the mind is not bad; it is a human emotion. But once we allow temptation and lust to take over, then the battle is lost. And that is when one becomes a victim of temptation.

Personally, when I find myself in a situation where I am being tempted, I think about my relationship. The first thing I think of is the love that is shared. I consider the energy and passion between us, and the thoughts of support and loyalty from my mate all comes to mind. And after these quick thoughts in reverence to my partner, I snap back to the consciousness of my commitment, but I am sure it is not easy for all, especially men. I will say flames can burn for a lifetime. If there are love and respect in the relationship, lust and temptation will not succeed.

The funny thing is- I was asked the other day why is it that you can hate more than one person, but you cannot be in love with more than one person? My answer was, "Unfortunately, you can." But to commit is to make a conscious choice of who you choose to be in a relationship with. Sometimes, we are not at liberty to fall in love with whom we want, and, depending on the circumstances, how many we fall in love with. But we have a choice to choose who we are going to commit to. To try and love and maintain a love affair with two people is unfair to those involved. And there is no real commitment until we pledge ourselves to one person. That is what makes the love special and causes a true bond to be shared between two people who intertwine as one.

True loyalty and affection is not a favor to be bestowed. We all deserve a relationship filled with trust, love, loyalty and honesty. Surely, every relationship has its rough patches at one time or another: mine, yours, theirs, and everyone's. There is no such thing as a perfect relationship. We should try not to place so much on our partner's shoulders to be everything- friend, lover, therapist, investor, and employee. Relationships are going to always have disagreements and arguments, maybe something you do not like. Some say it is mostly behind each other's habits as the relationship grows. However, disagreements are as intrinsic to committed relationships as sex. Sex is sometimes a big part of our strife, a lot of times mainly. Possibly, you are in one of those relationships that often argue and fight regarding sex. "Break up to make up." In other words, subconsciously, we do not fight each other to win. We fight to argue for power. Of course, we also fight for balance in the relationship. We fight to keep the relationship. If we do not argue and fight, we submit to surrendering and lose what is important: the relationship itself. I guarantee one thing for sure: The disagreement is definitely over if the bonding and lovemaking has begun again. Ups and downs arise in all relationships at one point or another.

Realism

As we journey through life searching for happiness and a person to share it with, we all sometimes can search and search and never find the companion we are looking for. We have preconceived notions about what kind of mate we desire. Most of the time, we are using our logical/better judgment side of us to help guide us in acquiring that special mate. After efforts of looking for that perfect someone, most will eventually concede by settling. Now, I will not say settling for less, but the word itself, simply settling, by not standing firm on your considered ideal mate, one who you believe will be instrumental to your way of life. This can definitely be damaging in many ways, for you and the person involved.

Personally, I would hate to be on the receiving end, as the one being settled for. Because I know my time may not only be limited, but I could possibly start to develop feelings, while in actuality, I am not the person's ideal mate or choice companion. Subconsciously, this will have an effect on both parties involved: the person that is settling and the one being settled for. First, it will affect the person who is settling for not remaining true to his/her ideas and desires, therefore establishing a form of mental strife stemming from his/her original expectations regarding the desired mate and how the requirements he/she yearned for are not being met.

Moreover, it eventually places one in a state of frustration and unhappiness. But, no one can say who is affected more. The person on the receiving end is subjected to the wavering emotions, and on top of that, he/she has possibly created feelings or perhaps more. To extend love that is not reciprocated is not love at all. So here you have one person who lacks happiness for not being true to his/her desires, and the other who is caught in the mix and possibly being placed on an emotional roller coaster solely from the energy that is being channeled from the source. So sure, I encourage excluding expectations and ideals when seeking companions/partners and to try and deal with each individual on a person-to-person basis, while finding the beauty that individual beholds. Being humans, we are all imperfect. It will be less stressful and fair to both parties involved in doing so.

However, I can offer another solution: Keep it real with yourself. By doing so, you will alleviate all the added stress and madness. If you find it difficult to adjust your life or change your ways and expectations, as you seem to embrace and understand them, do you! Do not change. Stand firm on your principles and beliefs. By doing so, you are ensuring your happiness by staying true to yourself, a state of being anyone can respect. It is only right to be true to our nature. Understand that in life you will find people that will hate, disapprove of, and will not always agree with your concepts and lifestyles.

So, I believe that the key is to be who we are, and do not sidetrack for anyone. Remain strong and never settle for anything other than the best for yourself. It is the surest way to grasp happiness in life, which calls for honesty. Honesty is important in any connection, whether friends, lovers, or otherwise. However, be assured that everyone is not privy to all information. So, one must exercise good judgment when sharing such details of his/her life, particularly when first getting to know a person, with the understanding that it is highly expected and required, providing the status of the relationship. Surely, as the connection grows, more layers of each person should be exposed and shared with one another. Keeping in mind, in early stages, you are not being dishonest because you choose not to share something. Express yourself honestly, by stating you're not comfortable discussing certain topics at the moment and that it would be better to discuss at a later date.

Any person can and will respect your decision, when presented in such a way, rather than being dishonest. The truth always comes to light, in the event a relationship blooms. So be real with yourself. If you are just looking to hook-up for the night, be clear. If you desire a solid relationship or marriage, express that. Most people are more comfortable with the friends with benefits get down. Whatever it is that suits you, be real about it.

People should not feel ashamed of who they are, things they like, and what is comfortable for them because if they are living their life for somebody else, they will never find happiness. If by any chance I am wrong for stating this belief, forgive me. Perhaps, honesty is outdated and over-rated. On the flip side, I am speaking about honesty from experience, coming from both ends of the spectrum.

In many relationships where the other person was dishonest with me in one way or another, I must say it did not feel great by any means, especially when feelings were involved. On the flip side, I also served in a bit of dishonesty. I must say that it feels much more liberating to be honest. Instead of being honest, most of the time, we become Smoke Blowers. That means telling the other person exactly what he/she desires to hear. That is more damaging than the truth by far. One of the most valued characteristics found in humans can be debated; however, that characteristic is said to be honesty. However, joyous or painful it can be, it is always required first and foremost.

Dishonesty requires so much more energy and thought than being truthful. Besides, maybe it is just me, but whenever I was untruthful, I felt like slum, by being fake instead of being real to myself. It is then that I started finding myself being more honest, almost to a point where it was becoming costly. Sometimes, it proved good; other times not so good, but the means justified the end.

Perhaps you are in a relationship, which has been going fine, and the two of you excitingly move in together. The family and friends are very accepting of your companion. After a few weeks, you start to notice little flaws, true deal breakers that you seemed to have overlooked. You decide you do not want to be in the relationship anymore. Not because things are bad, but because you are a different person now. People change in life. Sometimes, it is a phase. Inevitably, we are humans, and as human beings, we do change.

Would it be fair to hang in there because your friends and family adore the person? Would it be fair to hang in there to not hurt the person's feelings, all the while not being true to either of you? Again, you must not settle. And, you must keep true to yourself always. You must not consider what your family and friends think or have to say, and yes, pain may come about due to confronting your mate. Understand it is necessary to be gentle whenever you address the situation. But, you are obligated to express your feelings in a truthful manner, especially in these types of circumstances.

Realism and Settling

Realism of love is different by far,
No part-time friendships, I have to end from the start,
Not judging your ideals,
Accepting who you are.
When you fall to your knees,
Encouraging you to stand tall,
Regardless of the struggles,
Realism remains strong through it all.
Settling love is wavering, and
I refuse to relate.
When faced with tribulations;
They vacillate, and they shake,
Break, take and they fake.
Disagree with all you do, and
Never have a better way, what more must I say.
Now realism of love, I embrace that display.

Love and Abuse

As far as my memory takes me, I have always found the abuser of a woman the most unpalatable. I merely skirted the periphery as I touched the subject of abuse in the love section, with full intentions to elaborate my position on the matter in depth. I stand firm on my actions and words when I say a man should not allow any woman or situation to bring him to such a state where he is forced to abuse or harm a woman in any fashion.

This can really be a complex movement and must be aided by our women. I understand that a female's emotions are a bit different than a man's and can vacillate and be altered at any moment. However! Efforts should be made to assist in a non-abusive relationship. Speaking as a man, I understand more than you can imagine, how we are creatures of habit. But, physically abusing our women has to stop! Not just one particular group of men but all men: African, Caucasian, Latino, Arab, Asian, regardless of whether you are Christian, Catholic, Islamic or whatever you subscribe to in life. Whatever it is a woman is doing to a man that makes the man abuse her physically, it is something the man is not doing right.

Understand that we should have a more profound respect for our women in life, who are mothers, sisters, daughters, the parents of our seeds, and our companions. They are part of us in every sense of the word. As a man, I cannot imagine life without women. So yes, I do value a woman's essence and presence in every sense. As the late Godfather of Soul (James Brown) once said: "It's a man's world, but it will be nothing without a woman." I do not know how to express my feelings at this moment though, but I will try my best: To all women, I am overjoyed at the thought of you. Your essence is mesmerizing, and the thought is intoxicating in all aspects. For me to compose these thoughts is very necessary in hopes you take notice of a true male nature. As a man, it is my sincerest efforts to embark on this journey with you through life, as your confidant lover, provider and partner.

Sometimes, it is hard soaking up knowledge when it is coming from a woman, but they prove us wrong more times than not. And for that, I take notice and embrace their intuition with no hesitation. My manhood is not shaken when I admit that I am sensitive to their needs, nor do I find myself ashamed to say I possess a profound love to all women of the world. To say the least, it is because of women that I am inspired. It is not difficult for me to find beauty in them all, with the most incredible being their inner selves.

Women, you are accepted, and you are appreciated. I understand you little, and I understand you a lot. At any rate, you are acknowledged. I found very few things in life that can strike an emotional cord. Note: You are one. Your feminine ways shine on humanity a hundred fold, unique and amazing. I understand that the hearts of men can prove merciless in a vast amount. However, through your affection, I can be softened and soothed. Truly, my love and respect is more than mere words and can be seen in my deeds in time. And to all women who suffer or have suffered abuse at the hands of a man, I care if nobody else cares. And I hope you can find refuge in my words of truth! We live in demented times, though not all is lost. I admire your strength and courage. You do not have to wonder if I stand in your defense. I do! This is an excerpt from a poem I wrote:

"I am a King, and you are Queen to my throne,
You offer your heart and your love for the taking.
I promise the same, and it will not be forsaken.
These words that I speak are truth to the soul.
Nothing can compare to a love of our own."

Truly, we must find a solution to all the injustices and abuse that is being directed towards women all across the world.

I have no interest in reminding women of the abuse they have been put through. My effort is to reach both abused and abuser. Men, we must begin appreciating our women more. We must remain aware of the repercussions as a whole. Abuse only creates mental and physical disconnections. It distorts men's masculinity, not build it. We should be embracing women, not pushing them away. Until you can imagine trading places and witnessing that tragic circumstance, only then can you fully understand the harm that is being done.

Picture your heroine, your mother, a woman you admire most in life. Imagine arriving at her residence only to find out she has a swollen eye and her head is hung down with palms full of tears! Your emotions would be of fury and sadness, while at the same time being relentless in pursuit of revenge in her honor. My point is that all women should be treated how you would desire your mother or daughter or the woman you admire the most to be treated. We should understand life already deals a vicious cycle of ups and downs and also can be cruel in the most unimaginable way. My only request is that we become more passionate and eliminate the physical hostility. My opinion is if any man has to put his hands on a woman, then the two are better off without each other. In any disagreement or situation, communication is always key, and one should always leave a woman a choice. Just as men desire their mind to be respected, so do women.

As human beings, we evolve, and we no longer live in ancient times of dictatorship, but of times where each individual is free to think, free to live, and free to be him/herself. I find it absurd when humans begin to believe love is pain. A female should not have to tolerate abusive pain, only to love or experience companionship. Also the pain and abuse one inflicts destroys the psyche; therefore, a woman begins to refrain from opening up and expressing her more vulnerable side, sometimes eliminating a fair chance for a man deserving of her openness. All relationships do not start and end in battle. Love is to be beautiful, not abusive. And to all women, please take notice and appreciate men that are non-abusive, respectful, caring, and attentive to your needs. A lot of times, we can feel unappreciated and find it hard to express.

A word to all women who are taking the time to view my thoughts and opinions: Just because you have a good man or meet one does not mean he is a pushover or weak. Try to understand that many men still practice chivalry and are confident in their place as a man in a relationship. This as a product of hard-earned maturity that has evolved into selflessness and respect.

Please learn how to recognize these resourceful traits in men. It is a lot of effort that is being made to practice righteousness by you women. And one other issue, ladies: Men can find it rather disturbing when you give us the silent treatment. Rather than issuing the silent treatment and us getting nowhere, let us communicate about issues that are occurring. Even if you are not in the mood to talk, for the sake of the relationship, it must be done. By leaving us men in the blind, our minds can have a way of drifting to the worst. This is unhealthy in any form or fashion in regards to both individuals involved. This silent treatment does more damage than good. On the flip side, it serves as mental abusive toward men, which places men in a very inquisitive state of being. How are men to answer what they do not know?

Because the two share in a relationship, it should be mutual that trust be shared and neither should feel vulnerable in expressing thoughts and concerns that arise. I have seen many beautiful relationships end due to the disconnection that this silent treatment causes. Whether done consciously or subconsciously, it is a dangerous and destructive method. By all means, this should never be used as a tool to accomplish anything. We, as men and women, make a conscious choice to enter a relationship together. Surely, we enter under no false pretenses, no masks, and no negative motives. So ladies, I do encourage you to give us, men, the benefit. It would only serve a just purpose, mainly by working together as a unit. Then, identifying the problem that is disruptive to the energy that flows between us. Thereby, working together to provide a solution. Trust is important because it is required when opening up and sharing our feelings. So, it is very important that friendship be the foundation to every relationship. I am speaking for men, as a man, in regards to the topic at hand.

However, this is some information you ladies might want to take heed to. I composed this section on the subject of abuse. And at any rate, it goes both ways. My only hope is that this section and its contents achieve the intended purpose, which is to stop the abuse in relationships, and men and women together should acknowledge their wrongs and make them right. Enjoy life, enjoy love, and enjoy each other. Keep in mind always (abusers or losers), I stand firm.

Knowing How to Love

It seems that so many women are becoming more discouraged at the thought of men and love, because of false love in past relationships and from dealing with neglect and infidelity from men. In men's defense, in all my years of understanding, there is not such a thing as false love or real love. It is either love or it's not. In understanding, all men do not know how to love or express it to you, so forgive us. But unlike men, women are nurturers by nature, having an emotional caring and sensitive side naturally. Furthermore, love is demonstrated through actions and given in lessons, starting within the family as a child.

While teaching love to the male and female, the lessons were more directed towards the female, in regards to lover's emotions and sensitivity. Males were reluctant to embrace these ways and emotions, while considering these to be female traits. In addition, men are naturally raised to be masculine, an influential characteristic that is picked up by surrounding male friends and relatives, both peers and elders, as these are the ones assisting in the development of the young male mind state, setting the stage for adulthood. And in many circles, the majority of the time, affection is something rarely displayed once a boy reached eleven or twelve years of age.

So unlike women, men are not sensitive and emotional by nature. Men are more reactionary and most times have to be shown how to express these emotional traits. Simply put, if you desire to be shown love, show men and tell men how to love you, preferably through action. We men are very receptive and absorbing when a woman is being expressive. You will also find that many men are very expressive. You will also find that many men love but do not always know how to successfully express themselves. However, there are many men who desire to love and be loved just as much as women do, if not more.

At any rate, it just takes some assistance from the female, to help us men tap into that emotional side of us. And please, ladies, understand that while acquiring love from some men may be difficult, because of a strong upbringing of being exposed to masculine characteristics, men can also deal with security issues, just as women do. Men can also give their hearts just as women, if not more. When a man has extended his heart and fallen or given into love completely, he has then given up all power, not power over a women but power over self. To have one's actions controlled by emotions in scary, and I believe that is a fear that many men have thought of or are thinking at some point.

I know there has been a lot of discussion about giving and receiving love, more so concerning the likes and dislikes when loving a person and what is expected of a partner. Of course, each and every human being may have his/her own perception in regards to what love is. Love can be a subjective topic, and I have yet to hear of a love that relates to me, or one that I can relate to. And, I am sure there are others out in the world who can appreciate where I am coming from and understand my mindset. However, to even enjoy, share, or witness a love, one must first have a self-love, which is deep affection and appreciation for self.

In any event, to achieve the love of another or to extend love, loving self comes first. When engaging in any form of love, it can sometimes provide a path with no limits or borders. As for self-love and relationship love, it should not be difficult to differentiate. As for yourself, you should always consider what is best for you. At all costs, respect and appreciate your ideals and mindset. Sure, a lot of us may not do the necessary things we are supposed to in loving our mind, body and soul. Yet, our intentions are well placed in our best interest. The consideration you afford yourself, along with respect, are the basic concepts it takes to love any person. If you can grasp giving these qualities to another person, surely, you have self-love.

Keep in mind that it goes beyond just saying: "I love you." I always will believe that love is an action. Any human being can compose the most beautiful and most profound words, although when just mere words are spoken, any person can control the sun, moon and the stars. But when asked to perform, suffice it to say, the deeds will be inconsistent with the words. My point is there is no better way to receive love or extend love than by demonstration. Actions outweigh verbal expressions- any day of the year.

Ordinary Love

Love and admiration for all is something we should express daily- regular love in general. I know a lot of individuals misidentify love more often than not, as if love is limited to relationships. In actuality, it is a core emotion that is associated with more than just a feeling towards a companion or relative. I cannot help but notice when I look around the lack of love that is being demonstrated towards love of life, love of friendship, and love of humanity. Now, do not misjudge me. I am not some kind of love guru or love doctor professing to have always loved all. But, I have always possessed love in my heart, for more than just my companions and myself, but for my relatives, along with friends. I have loved many people in my life in many different ways, associates included. I have even shown acts of love to people I did not know.

Briefly let me say, I grew up around homeless and less fortunate people for years. And the fact is, the sight of the less fortunate always tugged at my heart and still does. And out of love, I constantly found myself offering food, giving money and sometimes conversation. You know – I stopped and shot the breeze, just for moral support. Even with associates and friends! Out of love, I would literally drag myself to assist in any matter or situation. These gestures were not done in search of self-gratification but solely on the basis of purity, out of respect and love for all.

With all that being expressed, it is my personal belief that people must have love in their hearts first, before anything. Self-love must exist before you, me or anybody else could love anything or anyone else. And once we do find that we truly show love for self, then we can embrace love in relationships. This is just my analysis.

Equality: Balance and Energy

The process of sharing and maintaining a connection takes balance and equality along with energy. Now, I will briefly go into why these elements are required, but first let me give my opinion on what should be a primary objective in looking for a partner. Start with a person who is able to engage in critical thinking and assist in decision making, while dealing with the daily problems that life presents.

Partners should always be considered when making a decision and should be able to aid when difficulties arise. A partner is there for help. It is a universal rule to be there in support of each other to make situations less complicated, and in the process, strengthening the unit and progressing as one at the same time.

I speak of this form of assistance based on issues and problems we face daily. Problems and constant issues can drain the chemistry and destroy the harmony that exists in the connection. Problems have a way of exasperating any relationship and test the strongest. Even when there is this great bond of extraordinary love, problems and complications will arise. In life, you will need a partner who is equipped to not only bring insight and assistance, but one to withstand the stress and anxiety that can be placed on you as a couple, as a team, and as a unit.

Stress and anxiety have destroyed some of the strongest couples and can break the strongest spirits. So in my opinion, if possible, search for a partner with a good state of mind, one that can be a great team player and knows how to make sound decisions. This goes toward both sexes, male and female. Now, something you may find helpful is to always make sure balance and equality are present in any connection that has been established. In any relationship, there is responsibility involved, and it is important that these responsibilities be equally shared. As with many things in life, there is always a balance that needs to be maintained to survive.

A lot of us humans can become so selfish that we completely forget about balance. If anything in life is unbalanced, it breaks down. It does not last, and this especially applies to partnerships. We all want and desire to be treated like queens and kings by a companion. Well, this is a two-way street. Even if the other person involved does not ask or demand it, it is a given that we should treat others according to how we want to be treated, more so in a relationship. It is an essential rule and a key to life with the intention of happiness as the ultimate objective.

So, the person should build us up, respect us, and share the same points of view in some cases. Even when the world cannot figure us out, the person understands. The point is- we all deserve happiness with a partner in life, and the balance should always exist and be equal. And beware, boredom can definitely become a destructive element if allowed in. Boredom is one of the main factors in creating infidelity and separation in a relationship. When I say separation, I'm referring to "mental distance." Now, I am not saying you have to become a magician or an entertainer, but find productive ways to keep monotony from surfacing.

Try accomplishing things together, such as goals and projects. Explore things with one another, discovering each one's likes. Keep the romance active; take trips with each other. It does not always have to be expensive. Consider places like museums. Even long walks along the beach can keep things romantic and interesting. Go out to dinner, keeping in mind variety and change is key. Mix it up (seafood, soul, Mexican, Italian, etc.). Movies are an option. There are always new films coming out. And if your pockets allow it, take trips. Excursions are always great to keep boredom from setting in. Even if it is just getting on the freeway and riding out to places and cities neither of you have been before. Adventure, excitement, all in one. Theme parks are always a good choice.

There are plenty of ways to keep a relationship healthy and exciting. Note that these few ideas and outings I named are basic, but they keep energy in the unit and assist in keeping the bond strong and growing. Also, they keep things from being destroyed by mental distance. Suffice it to say, it takes two for this to work while always staying focused on what is important to both. Embrace the experience and treat each day like the first with that same energy, passion and desire.

I found that one of the most rejuvenating things to do in a relationship is to travel abroad, whether the relationship is on the verge of ending due to boredom or not. Perhaps, you may want to build the bond and make it stronger. Whatever the case may be, trips outside the country have the effect of building and creating a new energy of trust and dependence on one another. Not to mention, the enjoyment of sharing the awesome experience with another heightens the romance. The fact is that you and your partner are together in a foreign country forced to cling to one another and become more dependent on each other, becoming more communicative, more romantic, and physically drawn closer. The isolation definitely plays a significant part in the connecting or reconnecting process. It is proven that seclusion and unfamiliar environments and places awaken the basic and natural instinct to attach to the one you are with.

Passionate Embrace

Passionate embraces, sweet taste of your kiss,
My heart is filled with love, and my mind in a state of bliss.

Walk with me through the darkness, and please hold tight,
Your love is my sunshine, and it provides me with light.

In this deranged messed up world, life deals to be so cruel,
So please don't be alarmed at the joy I found in you.

I know people can often wear masks and are full of games,
Though as time serves its purpose, your heart my love shall stain.

No dreams of illusions, false promises or confusion,
You inspire many emotions; it's rather hard to find a conclusion

In life, we find few that can be duplicated or traced,
Among those rarities where you passionately embrace

Breathing Room (Me Time)

In all relationships, love affairs and even marriages, both parties need "Me Time." That is personal time away from your companion. You know, room to breathe. Yes, it is cool that you are in love, and everything is going well. Keep in mind that nobody wants to feel suffocated. Speaking from a man's point of view, we do require some alone time or 'run the streets' time. And ladies, just because a man desires some alone time does not mean he is cheating on you. It is the same as how you women require your time with your girlfriends, sisters or relatives. That is "Me Time," away from your mate. Even when you go get your nails done or shop for a new fit that is "Me Time." Sometimes, you can sit around the house watching a movie or T.V. show or perhaps having a conversation on the phone. Believe it or not, that is "Me Time." And us men need that "Me Time," too.

Let us run the street. The majority of us might not need it, but many of us do. It is not that we are tired of our woman; we are just creatures that require remoteness on occasion. Other times, we may just want to hang out with the fellas. So, when a man goes off into another room and chills or wants to spend a couple of hours alone or with the fellas, ladies do afford him that luxury without any combat. A man you allow that free time to will be more attentive, at ease, more catering, and will love you better when he comes home.

To both men and women, I believe it is universal when I say neither of us likes to be overwhelmed or subjected to an over-imposing mate. To drown a person or make him/her feel imprisoned or smothered is one of the quickest ways to push anybody away. Let your partner breathe. And yes, I am sure this may not apply to everyone's relationship. If the love is tight, always keep in mind absence makes the heart grow fonder. Yes, even if the absence is just momentary. The heart and mind are two of the most mysterious organs that we may never fully understand.

Also, I do advise that we should always know our mate. Again, as I stated earlier, every relationship is unique in its own way, and every human being is different. Getting to know a person is a challenge. It is more complex than just knowing his/her favorite food, T.V. show, concerns about his/her lineage, or how many people he/she slept with. It is deeper than his/her past occupations or who he/she knows. I believe sixty percent of getting to know your partner is non-verbal. Yes, body language is underrated but speaks truth. The other forty percent is more in depth, such as whether or not a person's life is driven from values, morals and principles. Truly, you should inquire whether or not the person can deal with a sincere heart with you. To know your mate is to know he/she can be relied upon in any situation, even if that means letting someone else down for you.

These are questions that should be asked and qualities that should be looked for. Try and understand a person's soul and what makes the person unique from all others. Find out if he/she has a spiritual side and how it is. Does he/she have goals and what is being done to achieve them? Can he/she persevere through errors? Can he/she rise after failure? Believe me, this list can go on. These are the type of questions that need to be asked because this is a person we are trusting with our life and love. Whether or not one acknowledges it, when any of us commit, none of us go in looking to be let down. So, it is good to really know and feel the person out. There are going to be good experiences, and some will be bad. But always allow your heart to guide you. Study body language and ask in-depth questions to cut through the bullshit. In anything, I believe no one desires to have time wasted when looking to deal on a serious level.

PART TWO

Relationships

Opposites Attract (Bad Boys and Good Girls)

I am sure we have all heard the sayings, "Good girls like bad guys," and vice-versa, "Bad guys like good girls." Surely, it has much more to do with than just opposites attract. From an unbiased group of women, I conducted my own census. Some of the subjects were students, career women, and average everyday women. All were from different backgrounds and classes. The question posed was: "Do good girls like bad boys?" Conducting the census was a task. Believe me when I say it was not that simple compiling the answers. We all know that when asking about a preference, it may include many details and specifications.

Many of the answers did have one thing in common for certain: "An educated bad boy and business minded," came up along with "mental and financial stability." So, from my understanding of these women who were asked this question, their liking was not predicated upon the 'bad' in 'bad boy' but went further. It was not the 'thug persona' or 'street swag' that intrigued them; it was the totality of things. However, it is the bad boy swag that brings the edge into the relationship. The element that brings adventure is due to his down-to-earth and free-willed attitude. It is an excitement that keeps the adrenaline pumping off unexpectedly, always being surprised from the act of his free-spirited nature.

Also, women silently admire the projections of male dominance their man exudes when around other males and in general. The security women feel is indeed of great importance as was expressed profoundly while conducting this survey. These ladies also expressed how a man should treat them when in public and in private. That got deep! I will drop jewels on it later.

Furthermore, all the ladies did require special attributes: Primarily, the men should be able to adopt the appropriate behavior for any setting. They should know how to rock a fitted cap, jeans and boots, and turn around and get Dougie in a fine linen suit and dress shoes. You know-being able to go from street to corporate, and having good business acumen never hurt in the process. I, for one, have learned.

Another strong point that was made is fellas must be independent. You do not have to have a "King Abdullah bank account," but the ladies desire for us to be financially stable and can carry ourselves in any type of setting, whether it is her business party, dinner with family, etc. This means exposing layers of oneself. Ultimately, men should know women like a mix of street and book smarts.

Note for the men: Nowadays, many men fail to truly stimulate a woman sexually. And on the flip side, some women stand accused. First off, my dudes, sex is much more than an ad. More than an in and out, bump and grind, and it is over. Sex is passionate; sex is mental. It involves heavy eye contact, and body language is key. Understanding body language, sex is mental as well as physical. Foreplay is always instrumental. For instance, plant arousal kisses on her neck. Women love to be kissed on the nape of their neck. This is a sensual soft place to explore.

Follow that by some slight touching and breathing on her ear. This will send some women over the edge. Do not be afraid to caress her whole body and kiss her every place that has nerves: breasts, shoulders, belly area, rib cage, elbows, thighs, legs, feet, inner thighs, back of the knees, small of her back, spine, everywhere. Not one spot should be missed, and eye contact is a definite turn on for her. Do not be afraid to explore if she is interested in strawberries, grapes, honey, whip cream to ice cubes. Pleasure is unlimited. One should never be timid about tasting his companion. It is an ultimate pleasure; oral pleasure is always desired. Trust that.

With special attention applied to the clitoris, this type of foreplay allows her body to be fully in tune, making it easy for her to achieve an intense orgasm. As for intercourse, mix it up a bit. Be aggressive in your delivery but sensitive to her needs. Rough and sensual, but respect her body. Bite, spank, spice it up- if she is into it. Never let boredom or routine set in. This is for those who can use a few pointers, or just do not know how to adhere to a woman's needs. So, although it may be easy to get a good woman in your life, it is definitely an art to keep her.

Ladies, the same survey was conducted on the flip side. Asking why do bad boys or thugs like good girls? The answer I must say was unanimous. We all seek someone of regal and grace, a partner opposite of our imperfect selves. For an unknown reason, bad boys are indeed attracted to a quiet, educated female, who has self-respect and morals, and is strong minded yet still feminine. The fact is this type of woman gives a sense of foundation we sometimes desperately yearn. When we approach women, we do tend to seek a change or something that we may be missing. Simplicity and complexity in one, and innocence and the unknown together.

A man, any man for that matter, loves a woman who respects herself. She is found to be a challenge more so. Our mindset is often anything easily had is easily discarded, regardless of beauty. Sure, we love beautiful women, from beautiful eyes to the feet, the curves to the dips in the hips, lips, skin tone to the softness in her voice. A gorgeous smile is always appealing. Ultimately, ladies, do understand that nothing is more appealing than a very intelligent woman who conducts herself as a lady in public. However, in the bedroom, be sure to drop all inhibitions.

It is cool to bring the freak out. To all my ladies taking their time to read this, please feel me. I am going to share a few secrets with you and perhaps bring some insight to a few unanswered questions. I am sure that many women have heard the saying, "The key to a man's heart is through his stomach!" Not a chance, ladies. I assure you this is completely untrue. Yes, men like to eat, but this will never make a man stay home, devoted, or love you more.

The key is the mind. To captivate a mind is an art. Some of you ladies know what I am talking about. We very much admire the way you please us and are attentive to our needs. Believe me, that is a gift to a man. But to keep us is to captivate our mind, body and heart, and it starts with the mind. Also trust that there is nothing more intriguing than a woman who shows a little resistance.

Note: "Instant mind stimulant." Us men love a challenge by nature. So rather than surrendering, allow yourself to be conquered, and yes, we appreciate the time and effort you ladies put in to look nice and get dolled up. Sometimes, it is cool to get rid of the jewelry and make up. We men can appreciate your natural beauty. This is just some insight that you may want to know and might be helpful. Furthermore, it is in my nature to express only what comes to heart and what is true to me. If by any chance, anyone should feel offended by my writing, forgive me only if I have overstepped any boundaries, but not for expressing myself for being honest and true to myself. I find it difficult to not be authentic in my experiences, feelings and that which I compose.

It is fair to say that I love all women equally. Most importantly, I have a profound admiration and appreciation for the female gender. In my life's journey, I have never denied myself the experience of knowing and understanding women of different backgrounds, nationalities and social classes. African American, Caucasian, Cuban, Mexican, Puerto Rican, and all Latin women are yet different in many ways. Nigerian and Ethiopian women; Italians, Irish, and even Asian women, Chinese, and Korean. I have met Polynesian women, specifically Samoan.

Of all my encounters with these beautiful women of different languages and nationalities, who come from different parts of the world, I met all of them here in the United States of America. Surely, they may have different forms, skin tones to dialects, but one thing they had in common was that all of them desired a romantic, honest, ambitious, decisive, and diligent man. Those characteristics equate to power, protection, resources, and one who knows how to love. I pay homage to women for their many qualities. I say to all women- you are truly a gift. I thank the creator for a woman's existence constantly. I have loved women of different nationalities, and I hold no bias.

Note: For my sense of understanding beauty in life, I look to the form of a woman. I find all women beautiful in different ways, from style, manners, behavior, to her feminine ways. Beauty varies from the eyes to the lips to the tone of a woman's voice. The way a woman walks and her scent are all things of beauty. No woman offers the same company and pleasure. I had been in error to have once thought this as a youth. Surely, I have grown and have been corrected. The company and pleasure every woman gives are different in every way, and I find beauty even in the simple. I have never seen a more breathtaking sight. And in all my years, I have found nothing more splendid. This is just my personal opinion and feelings in consideration to all women.

Special Mate/ Security and Trust Between Each Other

You know, I can still remember my youth like it was yesterday. During my coming of age, when I grew up, male teens made "love" and "commitment" or showing any kind of affection to a female to be taboo. It was considered uncool if one developed feelings for a girl. To be laughed at for having feelings for a female was something I did not understand. You can say I ran with a rough crowd, along with being mature for my age. At the time, I was fifteen years old, a young gentleman by far, but thuggish as they come. I still could not understand this concept or mindset I was surrounded by. There I found myself not wanting to question the norm, while at the same time wondering if that was a way of life, growing up in all male teen circles. So, not really acknowledging the effect it had on me, I became a slave to my senses.

Though I thought I respected women at that time, I could not have been more wrong. I was not verbally of physically abusive in any way, but

I acted solely on the basis of not representing my true feelings and connection that I had with my partner and therefore, I looked at women only as beauty, sex and appearance. When in fact I would indeed have emotional feelings, but I would not bring myself to express them to her or anyone. This was all derived from this silly childhood male misdirection.

So despite my struggle with love, I always considered women to be the best teachers and critics in life. So, I went to my mother and explained the problem that was bothering me, and I remember it like it was yesterday. She said, "First off, you are allowing some childhood ideology to hinder you from making rational decisions as a young adult. Secondly, any male can insert his penis into a woman, but it takes a man to express himself, commit himself, and love a woman." I was eighteen at the time and will never forget that conversation.

So, I took heed and became more expressive and passionate with my relationships. Also, I could not help but wonder about past relationships. Maybe, I had come across my soul mate and did not recognize her. I do believe we all have a soul mate. Call me crazy, but we probably have more than one. You can find that a lot of times. Couples will be in love whether happily married or not, but consider themselves soul mates. Now, if for some reason one's relationship comes to a halt for any reason other than infidelity, I think a person can go find that same love in a different way, in a different person, and just maybe a greater love than the last, and go on to be with that person for the duration.

I am not saying one will find two loves the same. As with any love, each and every relationship has its own unique structure. But, I believe we as humans have more than one soul mate. Maybe it is just my personal concept, in keeping hopes that I did not overlook my mate, and if so expecting another will come along. One thing I am most certain of is we all deserve to be loved by somebody.

To all women and all men, I have learned you do not have to be afraid to express how you feel to your partner or in general. It is okay to give love and to be loved. And you will know when it is real. Many times, it comes with sacrifice and effort, to have a person that you can trust in your life, a person who knows all your passions, hidden secrets and desires, one who can understand your angers and feel what you feel and tend to censor what you censor. You know, someone you share an amazing unspoken bond. And even though love can be wonderful, beautiful, breathtaking and consuming, of all these things, keep in mind love can be simple and complicated at the same time.

Speaking on love, there is a point I will briefly touch on concerning trust and security. I am sure that many may not agree with what I am about to say, but again that is the beauty of having your own opinion. I know a lot of males like to take charge in all public situations, and there are women who rather show their independence, and some women do not mind a man always taking the lead when in public together.

Here is my opinion on the following scenario. Suppose a guy approaches a lady while she is in public with her man, whether it is to ask her status or to extend a compliment? Although her man is present, he is demonstrating security in his woman's responsibility to address and reject the approacher in a cordial and polite manner, sparing the guy a bruised ego with the politeness. Allowing the woman to take the lead not only shows security but trust in the relationship, and if by any chance the other guy ignores the woman's position, this is where her man steps in to take the lead and handle it accordingly. This is just a way of showing trust and security in the relationship.

For instance, a lady friend and I went out on a date. She was someone I had been seeing regularly for some time, so naturally feelings were starting to appear, specifically the trust had grown. So, on that date I decided to take her to a seafood restaurant located in Santa Monica where the service and food is great- I must say. We arrived and because reservations were made, we were seated immediately. (Memo to fellas- always reserve.)

Even though I am the one who gave our orders to the waiter, as a man, I always give the woman her independence and allow her to choose her meal, unless she asks for my assistance or recommendations concerning the food, as I may be familiar with the restaurant.

After being seated, we checked the menu out briefly. Ready to place our orders, the waiter came over. I took the lead and placed both of our orders. I did so solely because it is my belief that men and women both have their roles to play in public affairs and situations, and this shows stability in the relationship on behalf of both. Not long after, the waiter arrived with our meals. Because I placed the order, I was familiar with both meals. Off top, I took notice that my date's meal was incorrect. Again, it is and was my duty to rectify the incorrect order immediately. So, she not only showed stability but trust in our relationship by allowing me to handle such matters.

Some may consider it irrelevant, and perhaps, I am a bit old fashioned. I do find myself still practicing chivalry. You know opening doors for women, always ladies first. I pull out chairs for women at restaurants, just to name a few. But on the flip side, to make my point in regards to the "Trust and Security," check out this next demonstration while in public. So, back on track.

We left the restaurant after dinner and went down to the Santa Monica pier. Both of us, as outdoors people, entertained ourselves with the sight of the ocean, the breeze, all the lights, games, and snack bars everywhere. I could not begin to tell how many people were there, singles and couples, but it made for a lovely scene and somewhat romantic as well. So, we played a few games, while at the same time, enjoying each other's company. Not to mention, the view and the vibe was great. We decided to grab some cotton candy- at her request, of course. While at the cotton candy stand window, I took notice that a guy was eyeing my date. So being secure with mine, I chilled as he approached her. He complimented her look and in a regular tone asked if she was single and if they could exchange numbers.

As a youth, there was a time when I would have acted a fool, but I have matured, which is good. Anyway, him not seeing me, I recognized the entire situation. And, I admired how my date addressed the situation as a lady. She responded that she was involved and was there with a date, while pointing to me showing acknowledgement. By her handling the situation in a polite manner, the rejection was not taken hard and spared his ego in the process.

By that time I was fully engaged, understand that if by any chance he would have gone any further, after she asserted her position, then I would have intervened and taken the matters into my own hands, with a more direct and masculine approach. Case in point, taking the position I did allowed me to display trust and confidence in not only my mate but myself as well. Also, it kept her empowered with her independence, by trusting she could handle such situations.

It is always in both mates', males and females, interest to leave each other a choice. Whether it is to make decisions or faking the lead on certain things. Equality is a great way to display respect along with trust.

I hope my point was made, and at some point, you felt where I am coming from. In closing, I am a firm believer that if you cannot trust or feel secure with somebody, it is hard to be with him/her. Almost all the time things will fail. It just simply will not work. So, I hope that a lot more couples start building their level of trust and security in their relationships.

Long-Distance Relationship Survival

For quite some time now, I have struggled with maintaining a long distant relationship. In the process, I came to realize there is no guarantee in surviving the distant currents, while dealing with the different physical and emotional swings one encounters along the way.

Sometimes, this distance can assist in making the heart grow fonder, true. Yet, keep in mind that too much absence or distance can destroy the strongest connection. Certainly an attempt at keeping the heart's fondness towards one another requires undeviating obligation. The reason I chose this topic for discussion was due to the many loves and relationships that exist in this current era we live in.

I find many men and women are struggling to survive distance. Many are those who have spouses/partners who are away on leave, during these times of war and chaos, mainly military personnel, but this phenomenon is not limited to them. Whether it is concerning armed service men/women overseas or one who is out of town due to careers or business, prison included, or perhaps school (across the country, or at a university of some sort), whatever the situation, there are many individuals that face this plight. Therefore, it is in my efforts to express and share a few ideas and methods that have worked for me and a companion I once had. Perhaps you may find these methods applicable in your journey concerning the distance and absence you may face.

First off, if you have witnessed any part of this lifestyle, you fully understand it can, many times, serve as being stressful. To overcome the duration, understand it takes devotion first and foremost. One must be dedicated to making and keeping a continued support base with each other. This definitely requires energy from both persons involved. If I can best offer an action one needs most it would be sacrifice. Dealing with all the lonely nights and the withdrawal of being without one another surely has a way of testing one's spirit, from the missing companionship. The only means of survival is a constant mental connection of development when the physical is absent. The mind becomes the most valued and strongest means of togetherness.

Before I go into depth on the basic key elements, I would like to say, keeping oneself occupied while separated can serve in a very therapeutic manner. Keeping the mind and the body active in productive ways can serve as a true distraction. Temporary separation will sometimes produce stress, anxiety and frustration among other things and can be unhealthy. So, here are some key elements none of which should be taken lightly.

Note: Every method should be demonstrated from both parties equally for the relationship to stand the test of time. It will take more than the word love; it takes actions. Actions should not be limited but maximized in all given aspects. Greeting cards, for example, always bring a smile to the face with the sweet connotations that are inside. They are meaningful, sincere and perfect for those who do not like writing. And for the recipients, the card is always a gift in itself.

Letters, on the other hand, have a way of displaying oneself. They bring a more personal presence and are sufficient enough to extract deep feelings of love. In letters, we are allowed to be ourselves, and they will be much more appreciated from the fashioning of our words and thoughts. Overall, letters are priceless and undervalued. Letters are a form of romance. They are private thoughts shared between the writer and the reader. Both are at ease and have no concerns of strain or opinions. If I must add, when I was involved in a distant relationship, it was greeting cards being exchanged and occasional phone conversations.

But letters, on the other hand, had a more gravitational pull towards me in every sense of the word. I began literally to expect the mailman in hopes to receive a letter from the person. And yes, the feeling was equal and mutual in every way. In every response, I took pride in being completely expressive with every letter. Keep in mind this played a major role in surviving the long distance between the two of us and should be applicable with any couple or friendship subjected to these terms and conditions.

On the flip side, I know many of you are less inclined to write letters and may feel it is a bit old fashioned. Yes, it is true. Times have evolved into a more technological era, with fax machines, cell phones, texting, photos, social connection sites, etc. However, some of the parties involved may be limited and not have access to some of these tools. One thing is for sure, everyone does have access to a telephone, whether it is a phone booth or cell, which brings me to one last element I will share.

I discussed how greeting cards are good. I have also expressed how letters are great and sentimental. Last, but not least, the exchanges of phone calls can hands down be the most fulfilling interaction when faced with a long-distance relationship. They create an environment that relaxes you, and yet gives you the power to be able to extract many emotions at once. Communicating by way of phone tends to be more poetic, more intimate. Just the sound of your companion's voice, which you have yearned to hear due to physical absence, can indeed create sparks, placing you in a briefly enraptured state of being. It should feel normal if the sound of each other's voice provide a source of tranquility and sustainment.

Do not under any circumstances censor your words or emotions. Intensity is always great. It builds energy and makes for a comfortable conversation. Every topic should come into play. No feeling should be withheld, especially if you are a couple. A little phone romance should not be excluded as an option. It is definitely a way of long distance bonding. Of course under no pressure, as both individuals would have to be interested. Surely, this is reserved for those special connections. Believe it or not, such attention does please.

I am most certain that a lot of you out there are probably familiar with all that was said. But many are not, so here are just a few ways of overcoming distance: At any rate, as with anything in life specifically relationships, nothing is guaranteed. But that should never deter a person from exploring the joys of connecting. My focus and mission here was to extend a few methods that I found to be very productive, not just to me but to many others. Surviving the test of separation is very possible, challenging but possible. Again, it starts with security and willpower to be together. And in regards to ourselves, when dealing with this long-distance relationship, we must already be of a focused and confident mindset, a complete person if I must say, not a person looking to be complete. The reason I make that statement is that it takes a certain type of patience, a spirit of serenity and discipline.

There are three attributes a complete person demonstrates. Nevertheless, if an easy fight for love is what you are seeking, this is not it. It is a battle indeed, and one must be mentally and fully prepared for it. Know that some of the greatest things and achievements in life are obtained by a duration of sacrifice. So, if you are one of those individuals in life that is witnessing a similar situation, I say to you 'fight,' especially if you feel it is worth the battle. Truly, it is a choice that you and your partner will make. All that I encourage is let your heart guide you, and only make moves when your heart is in it.

All in all, it is very possible to have and overcome. I am speaking first hand as the prime participant in developing and surviving a love in long distance. It was a classic love tale if I must say so myself. It was with a companion whom I was with for six months before the distance separated us physically. Things were great. We were in love, and we could not have been happier together. However, we both had different paths in life. By her career sending her abroad, it forced us to nurture a long-distance relationship. It took energy, passion, patience, love, communication, desire, and much more than strength. But through the methods that were stated, we survived four years. So, believe and try. Do not be afraid to experience romance "Skype Style" for distance. You will love it.

Open Relationship

There was a time when relationships were established with respect. Marriage was also founded on respect and pride. As a matter of fact, you had couples that could not wait to announce their engagement to their parents, relatives, or close friends. The same is true with finding that special person and creating a relationship. It was a joy, a respect, surely something to be proud of. In some cultures, it was frowned upon for a woman to not have a respected man in her life at a certain age. And most times, it also included marriage. The same would also be applied to the males, just in different volumes and fashions. But the man indeed was expected to have had a nice respectable woman with family oriented qualities. Men were also expected to have stability. It was not only expected but considered a way of life in regards to manhood.

Now these same expectations that were exercised in both, the male and female psyche once then, seems to have deteriorated by the day. So, thinking back to those particular ways of life, it is completely different in today's relationships and values on a grand scale. Sure, there are still values, respect and sacred bonds of marriage being created. In contrast, there are so many relationships that display a void and emptiness, which shows how we in society demonstrate our detachment from one another-consciously and subconsciously. It is more psychological than anything. How are we not to act in such a purely lustful manner, when that is all we are exposed to? Reality T.V., music, Internet, and all forms of entertainment contribute to our habits and way of life. Swingers, hooking up, open relationships and friends with benefits do the same. Now, I am not judging, if these suit your lifestyle. The point is- let us not allow the media to dictate the abolishment of love and commitment. The lack of love and passion is very much visible although they are much needed in these times.

Speaking of swinging, I once was given an option to participate in an open relationship with a past companion. Now, I really do not know where this concept was derived from or what its purpose was to accomplish. I have had friends subscribe to this lifestyle. I have even heard of celebrities indulging in this open relationship lifestyle. However, when I was asked to consider this invitation, I could not even wrap my thoughts around the idea. For reasons such as men are territorial, and I myself am a territorial person and private. Not in the sense as though a woman is my property, but the fact if I am with this person, we should consider our bodies being given to one another as a gift. What is the point of a relationship if it is open? I am a selfless individual but not in regards to sharing my companion; besides, I find it hard for me to detach from my emotional side while knowing my companion/mate is having relations with another. I could not bring myself to consider my feelings and acceptance to revisiting the flame that once was. These would burn out immediately. In short, nothing is sweeter than a love of your own.

I believe we all have a gift, and that is to share ourselves with that special someone. It is bad enough that it is so easy to fall in and out of love. Surely, I could not love my companion after knowing she has given herself to another. As for my partners, to engage in a self-serving fantasy, such as an open relationship or swingers, is to turn a blind eye to love.

Quality Time and Affection

Many relationships have been helped by talking to a therapist. Now let us be real, the majority of people would rather not spend money on that service or do not have the money for that service. Building a connection and establishing your relationship a lot of times can be complex. Put simply, give quality time.

Note- That does not consist of being with the kids or sitting around the house. This also does not mean attending clubs, parties, or get-togethers. Quality time consists of just you and your mate, whether it is going to the park to relax together, feeding the ducks in the pond, sharing a long walk along the beach together or quiet scenic spots that may produce a beautiful sunset. Just be creative when creating that quality time between the two of you. Wherever you decide, have loose conversation while you bask in the ambience. Nothing stressful should be brought into the equation. It is about a relaxing, peaceful time. Enjoy pleasurable, honest, intellectual conversation if any.

Quality time is another way to stimulate love or heighten the chemistry. There is something about alone time with a person that ignites energy like a gravitational pull, and this is not just for new couples, but for couples who have been together and things are a bit shaky. Because we are human and our mind and ideals change constantly as we grow, it is natural to have a love or attraction that is brief. However, if your position is to fight for the longevity of that relationship, it requires spending quality time. It's a building and a rebuilding stage, minus the added distractions.

Anytime one is in a love affair, relationships, friendships, etc., it should be treated like a plant. If you are invested, you know what is expected. Just as a plant needs sunshine and water, without that time being put in for care, it dies. The same is true with us. We must give each other that time. Presence is the sunshine! And communication is the watering! Do not laugh! I am being real. Think about how many friendships, good friendships, which were lost by the wayside. Not because of bad terms, but simply due to lack of time spent together and the lack of communication. Distance is current if an existing couple does not pull in time.

I mean seriously. How can you expect to develop when you lack quality time? And about that saying, "Absence makes the heart grow fonder!" That is true only when the relationship has been welded in time and found to be secure. Until then, absence only creates distance, depending upon the amount of time absent. The crazy thing is we are living in a new era, an era of hook ups and technology where quality time with companions are becoming minimal. If you find yourself spending more time on the internet than in your relationship, don't be surprised if things are not as strong as they could be. See the funny thing about time is that it creates! Whether it creates good or bad is solely up to us. The objective is to create good, such as passion and concern.

Love and Affection

This section is in regards to even those who have created relationships online. And the same applies once you have found out this person is not a psycho or a creep, thus having the potential of becoming a respectable companion. Push away from the computer, and get out there to spend some time with the individual. Only then are you going to fully recognize the person's true being.

So I say, get out there and spend, some personal time with each other male or female. Make sure the first few dates or meetings are conducted in public places- just to air on the side of caution. Besides, you want to know who you are you dealing with. I am sure no lady wants her time wasted. So, take action by putting in the time to get a true sense of the person, to see if this is for you. Remember, time creates and time builds...

Dating Tips

There are millions of human beings who go through everyday life afraid to date because of the lack of basic fundamentals. Or, possibly they are dating and still can use a few basic tips on do's and don'ts. One would be surprised at how many people struggle with dating or even just getting a date. We can research tips off the internet or buy a how-to-date book from a scientific point a view. There were a few I found a bit interesting. However, I am here offering tips from a different perspective, from your average every day person. Extending tips from experience, I am one who thinks like you think, considering what you consider and go through what you go through. Most importantly, I understand where you are coming from, as I come from the same place.

I will be sharing a few tips for both sexes. I believe males should know a few do's and don'ts when dating. The same is true for females out there. Before I drop a few jewels, please note, this is by no means a form or fashion of criticism to neither sex. It is only a short interpretation of expressive minds from both men and women.

Men's Tips: Do's and Don'ts

1. Fellas, when we step to a woman, it must first and foremost always be with confidence, as if you are representing the masses. Surely, no woman likes a man who is unsure of himself. So, whenever you step to any lady, be confident, relax, and just be yourself. Being yourself is important. Just the way you can sense fake friends and associates, women have that same ability, knowing when a man is not being authentic. So, leave the rapper/actor persona out of the picture. Always remain confident. Nothing comes to a scared man but a dream. Be yourself always. Do not be ashamed of being appreciated for who you are.

2. Grooming, Hygiene, and Appearance. These indeed may cause a bit of controversy, but I must bring the real. Hygiene is very important. This goes far beyond impressing a woman. One should practice good hygiene in general. But sticking to the mission, do not expect to receive any action with a body odor and/or bad breath. And that does not mean go drown yourself in cologne. Always shower or bathe daily. And keep your breath fresh always. I am sure everyone brushes before they leave the house, but during daily routines, you are out eating, drinking, etc. Keep some Double Mint or Winter Fresh gum on you.

Grooming is another important factor. Stay groomed if you are going on a date. Even if you are planning to go meet a woman, nails for one must be clean! Women dislike a man with dirty nails. Also, keep your hands moisturized. Think about it, a woman is going to picture you touching her, and if your hands look like you have been working on engines just thirty minutes ago, you can forget it.

Lastly, dress to impress. Appearance matters a lot, from coordinating your colors to the cleanliness of your shoes. I am not saying show up in expensive clothing, but know how to dress. A woman always checks out a man's attire, shoes included. A lot of times this can be the determining factor for whether you get the number or not. So always maintain good hygiene, keep grooming standards up, and always dress to impress.

3. Whenever you meet or approach a woman in an attempt to ask her out or get acquainted, do not come with a rehearsed line that sounds like game. And do not call her out her name. Example, "Yo, Ma!" "Hey, sexy!" or "What's good, boo?" Trust and believe, all women are not accustomed to that. So a simple hello, extend your hand, and introduce yourself. Show her that chivalry is not outdated. Remain courteous and polite in your conversation and be respectful. If she is not interested, tell her to have a nice day and push. That means leave in style, with character. But keep in mind, women love a man who knows how to address and talk to a woman. Basically, they respect a man who steps to them correctly and politely, with no games, just being honest and real. Again a simple hello, extend your hand politely, and introduce yourself. That is how we step on a grown man tip.

4. Men, whenever you have made a good connection with a lady and the conversation is flowing or at a standstill, do not ever spread yourself thin by imposing your life story, starting from childhood to present. You cannot only bore but scare a woman off. You also take away all mystery from yourself. You are no longer intriguing.

Along with that, keep conversations of finances and personal possessions out of the conversation. No need to discuss how much you are worth, or how many vehicles or pieces of jewelry you have. This can definitely be seen as tacky and a sign of insecurity. Besides, if she is interested in your bank account and not you, get out of there quickly. You are with the wrong date. Do not take away your mystery by sharing your life story, and whatever money you make or have, keep it to yourself - real talk!

5. It is common knowledge that all men at one point or another think about a female's ex-encounters. In regards to relevance, it does not have anything to do with you or the present moment. Many men may be familiar with this rule, but a lot are not. So, do not under any circumstances ask a woman about her ex or exes. Allow her past to remain hers. Besides, it is possible you could be stirring up old feelings, whether good or bad. And that is counterproductive to you achieving a successful dating experience. On top of everything, nothing should matter but you and her. So, do not ask about a date's ex-encounters. It is not productive for either of you. So, let the past be the past, and keep it moving.

6. Do not make flirtatious remarks about another woman when with your date. This is definitely seen as disrespectful and inconsiderate by far. So even if you see another attractive woman, it is cool to glance on the low quickly. But do not verbalize any comments under any circumstances. Respect the one you are with.

7. Don't be cheap. Whenever going out on a first date or second date, it is important to not be cheap. Keeping in mind you are in the preliminary stages and would like to leave a nice impression on her. So always try and choose a great restaurant when going out to dinner or lunch. Being frugal should be the farthest thing from your mind, and being that it is early in the stages, it is always good to pay even if she chose the restaurant and offered to pay. Sure, it is cool to share the tab on dates down the line. But, in the early stages, it is on us, men. Don't be cheap and always leave a nice tip. It says a lot about a man.

8. Last, but not least, expressing jealousy. Whenever I am on a date, personally, I love when a date of mine receives attention. So, whenever you are in public with a lady you are dating, expect men to admire. Do not get upset by showing jealousy. She is there with you not the other guy or guys who are looking at her. Besides, it should, in turn, boost your ego. As long as you and your date are not disrespected, all is well. Carry on.

So, there you have it: eight steps that can prove useful to the inexperienced dater. And, I hope by all means they will assist everyone. Sure, there are lots of rules on do's and don'ts when dating. I felt the need to point out a few that happen to have been in recent discussions with some male and female acquaintances.

Women's Tips: Do's and Don'ts

Now, we begin with women on a few tips, some do's and some don'ts. However, this is in no way criticism. Just a little heads up when dating, concerning some things that are on men's minds.

1. Do not be afraid to relax. In any situation where you are on a date with a guy, try and relax. When you are relaxed, it definitely eases a tense environment. The two of you are getting to know one another, so it is helpful to receive answers from you that consist of more than one word. We all know what I am talking about. A lot of times guys fight for conversation by asking a hundred questions, and ladies will offer one word answers (yes, no, maybe, etc.). I must say that can be discouraging in a way. And, it leaves a man blinded. So, just so you women understand us men better, we are reactionary creatures by nature. We feed off a woman's vibe and energy. So, do not be so tense. Relax.

2. Do not compare. Men in general will put up with a lot of things. I mean really. Men have pretty thick skin and are very tolerant. But women

should never compare a man to another man, especially your ex, and please do not bring your ex up in conversations. This is one quick and sure way to turn a guy off. Even if you think you are being subtle. For instance, "Oh, John used to bring me here for dinner," or "Shawn used to love ordering the steak. You should try it." No! This is annoying and insulting in a major way. If this does happen to take place, do not be surprised if your date excuses himself to the restroom and never returns. So, ladies keep your comparisons to yourself. There will be much better interaction, without the ex on the date with the two of you. Besides, it creates unnecessary tension.

3. Do not overdo appearance on accessories. Ladies, we love the fact you take pride in your appearance. We men can appreciate a woman that likes to look nice. You know hair, nails done, outfit looking nice with nice heels, sandals, etc. But sometimes, other things can be overdone. Not bashing! But all the heavy make-up, extended eyelashes, and excessive jewelry takes away authenticity. We men are simple creatures and can appreciate natural beauty. Furthermore, do not worry about brand name clothes that have no meaning to men. To be honest, the only brand name we love is Victoria Secret. Seriously, do not overdue appearance with accessories.

4. Jealousy. This is not becoming of a lady. It shows insecurity within self. Women are going to notice your date if he is attractive. Furthermore, if you two are at dinner and a female waiter is acting in a light flirtatious manner, do not act out in a jealous rage. Do not show contempt towards your date for not being rude to the waiter. He is right for being polite and remaining professional. If he is feeding fuel to the flame, then most certainly it should be addressed. Other than that, he is with you.

5. Modesty. Surely, today women are accustomed to nice things, meaning expensive nice things, and men do tend to show their appreciation by

treating a woman- buying her gifts. Whenever a man does offer to purchase you a gift, do not require the most expensive, because he can afford it. This can create distance in men. On the flip side, if you do not feel you have the will to refrain from the most expensive, allow him to choose. In most cases, it is a win-win for you. A man would generally take it upon himself to shower you with a well-respected gift anyway. By taking this approach, it eliminates that situation from arising. So, I say respectfully to those who do not practice it: "Show some modesty."

6. Profanity. We are all adults and profanity gets used, which is cool. But when out on a date, do not over exaggerate as though no other words exist. Men want a lady not a sailor. Too much profanity from a lady can be a turn off.

7. Do not use your phone unnecessarily while on a date. This can be rather irritating. Ladies, do not constantly answer your phone while on a date, unless it is an emergency. This issue is irritating and can be received as a sign of disinterest. However, all phones should remain on vibrate for both parties when out on a date. Because a date is planned, the schedule should be respectfully cleared for that given time. What we men consider use is when you make or accept recreation calls, showing no importance and clearly disrupting the atmosphere. It may be looked at as small to you. However, it breaks a connection that one is trying to build, kind of like if you are handling important business on the phone and the other person keeps telling you to hold on to answer the other line. It gets annoying and can be distracting. It's the same feeling. So please ladies, spare men on dates. Please keep the phones out of the picture, unless an emergency arises.

8. Timing. Be on time. When going out, especially on first dates, some women can, a lot of times, not be ready when the date arrives. We

understand you desire to look your best, or you are double-checking your attire or hair. Honestly, a man loves a woman who is on time. This, ladies, is a quality that is really appreciated. With all that said, ladies I am compelled to close. It is pretty much small things that matter to men. Overall, a woman is a blessing, and this will conclude the few do's and don'ts in the dating stage, for the inexperienced.

In regards to males and females, I am certain both would like to leave an impressionable mark after their initial engagement. Hopefully, this can be of some assistance. So, go over this about ten times, and you will find yourself ready to establish your mark by applying a few of these concepts or understanding some concepts of the opposite sex. Whichever way this is used, just do not misuse it by not using it.

Courting

Whenever in the dating scene, understanding courtship and the way it works is important. Courtship is a well-known method and way of life in pursuit of a mate. You do have male and female courters. Courtship is just a process of courting with a view of a relationship, trying to win affection or favor from a person. This term or behavioral action is nothing new and has been practiced for hundreds of years and is still relevant. It is merely a charming tool to obtain favor with the person you are seeking.

As I said, you do have both sexes. Men and woman have their own styles of courting and the thing about it, it is universal. Now truth, there is nothing wrong with this action. I am sure we all desire to obtain favor from the person we are pursuing to be our mate. However, appreciate it when the courting is dealt in truth. Understand a courter can deal in truth or in falsehood. And when it is dealt in falsehood, it is known as the courtship of a puma.

I believe each and every adult who has been in a relationship has courted or been courted at one time or another. Not that this is some unique power, but it is about getting to know a person and trying to obtain favor with him/her, while attempting to enter his/her world. And let me say, at first, any two people can be reluctant to believe the other's words and refrain from opening themselves up. Only because it can be difficult in determining what is true and what is false.

Do allow me to point out how the superficial works. We are going to call it courtship of a puma. In establishing favor, one makes complete effort to spend quality time with you, whether it is just sitting around or going out. They design their schedule to be compatible with yours, while remaining attentive to all your needs. Most of the time, they are so enraptured that they take the initiative on certain needs, even desires. In every effort, they show high levels of support, accepting your perfections and flaws. They demonstrate signs of loyalty, respecting all your concerns as well. They are humble, polite, and demonstrate all the qualities we look for in a partner. Most importantly, they constantly insinuate a perfect love and how they possess that quality. Keep in mind, these are from both ends of life: male and female. If I must say so myself, who would want to pass up an opportunity like this, to finally find such qualities in a man or woman, to be treated with such passion and attentions? It is hard to not embrace a person who offers such things. I mean really, we all look to be number one in somebody's life while treated as if no one else on the planet exists.

However, once the connection has been established and the puma has secured a spot in your life, it is then you will notice a change. Surely, I am not the only one who has witnessed this several times in this day and age. But it is like the courter/puma reverts: All the respect and consideration go out the window. The manners that were once demonstrated are no longer practiced, as if they never existed. Attitude starts to become distant and moody, so irrational that you would start to think your partner or that person is bi-polar. However, they are far from bi-polar; it is all part of them reverting to their original form and truest self. And now all interactions and communications become more and more disagreeable. Quality time is obsolete.

Do not be surprised if you feel alienated in the relationship. The reason is it is a sham; superficial in its purest form. A lot of suitors put on a sham only to achieve its intended target. It is a game to say the least. You should know things are highly unlikely to change, and the best thing to do is to shake it off and walk away.

On the flip side, when you encounter one that deals in truth, cherish that as long as possible. I must say, it is becoming rare in this era to find a person who practices loyalty and who says what he/she means and means what he/she says. And that is unfortunate, though all is not lost. It is my belief that things can change for the better. I am speaking on pure instincts and experiences. A lot of what I speak about I believe I am right in my own mind, but surely one will be judged for whatever he/she says or believes. So, I humble myself and take the risk of being wrong to some people, but true to myself. Be aware of the fake and always cherish the real.

The Duality of Parenting

To everyone who is reading this book- ask yourself how many single parents you have met in the past twenty-four months, both men and women. Although the numbers for single women are staggering, do consider both sexes. Now let me say this, when men and women bring children into this world, a relationship is no longer casual, but should be at that point considered serious. Things should transcend into a unit for the sake of the child. It took male and female both to create, so indeed it takes both to nurse, raise and guide the child. We all have heard many excuses of why either one of the parents is not in the child's life. However, if the parent that is absent is not abusive, deceased, incarcerated, or a bad influence, that parent should be present. I believe any issue is repairable for the child's sake.

The point I am trying to make is it takes two to parent. Sure, it is proven a man can raise a child by himself, but there are things that only a woman can teach a child (both girl and boy), and sure it is proven a woman can raise a child who aspires to greatness, but again there are things only a man can teach a child. Both parents provide necessary traits and lessons on life and experiences. Yes, I am 100% man, thanks to both parents. My father showed and taught me a lot of things, and my mother contributed the same amount, if not more. I believe that the woman is the foundation, and the man is the structure, and both of them create a harmonious and cohesive balance in the household.

Not taking anything away from a man teaching, but my mother was the one who told me the basic principles of love and affection. Perhaps it is the innate, instinctive nurturing characteristics of the female. My mother taught me how to address a woman, manners, and how to think rationally, among many other life lessons. My father taught me respect, dignity, honor, nobility, principles, the values of hard work, pride and humbleness. He taught me how to be a man and a gentleman. He showed me how to defend myself and my family. He gave me hands-on training of how to repair a bike's flat tire to a car's mechanics to appliances, everything around the house.

My point is both parents are needed. Whenever a son or daughter needs advice from a parent who is not there, either they go to someone else looking for answers, knowledge and understanding, or simply learn from others or experience, which in some cases serve as the good teacher. But in other cases, that can be detrimental and put the child at a disadvantage, speaking from experience.

Having seen women raising children on their own, I find myself supportive in their plight. Having sisters and a mother of my own gives me the authority to speak on this matter along with a love and respect for the youth. My sister, being a single mother herself, had given birth to a handsome baby boy, my nephew. Now just around the time her son was stepping into the potty training stages, she and the child's father separated, placing her in the difficult position of being a single parent, having to fulfill the roles of father and mother. She was faced with trying to teach her son how to stand, aim and urinate properly as a young man.

This can be real pressure on any male child to have a woman instructing him on how to use his tool. Trust me, this is a class best taught by a man. I am certain that any young male child would dread the experience of a woman guiding in this subject, and I am sure it is just as frustrating the other way around.

So, I felt the need to enclose a brief eye opener: a notation on parenthood. Specifically, I want to encourage both parents to sacrifice for the child's sake. I understand how times are changing fast. We are living in a world where technology is present and quite often absolutely necessary in daily living. Also, we are exposed to the hook up culture and a political climate where the politicians are more concerned with partisans and selfish interest than the best interest of the people and the country. I am scared to think about what we are evolving into.

So, I request, let's not abandon traditional, instinctive morals, love, respect, and humanity. Let us all remember that in order to be human, we must first be humane. Let us remember that our children are our future, and I will be the first to sacrifice my own interests in order to preserve theirs. That is just a word to all the parents and parents-to-be out there. My dad once told me: "Always do your best. If you fall, get up and keep going. Persevere. Never give up." Let us push the youth to strive for greatness. There is a purpose and a space in this world waiting for us to carve it out.

PART THREE

Purpose and Passion

In all relationships we enter, we go in accepting the person just the way he/she is. Perfect or imperfect, we embrace that individual, along with his/her dreams, goals, ideas and concepts. Surely, we must exercise patience, and never are we to be more persistent in supporting one another. Over-persistency is very damaging, a point I anticipate discussing, to shine some light on to show how this can destroy a relationship, sometimes before the connection is even made.

Many of us have dreams we desire to fulfill, and we work for them, along with having goals we aspire to accomplish, which we also work towards. I find that many people do not extend the support a partner needs. Believe it or not, a companion's opinion and support is highly needed when striving to reach a goal, regardless of whether it is asked for or not. Out of respect and courtesy, one should offer support to his/her partner. One reason is to point out the two of you are a unit. What affects one, affects the other, whether good or bad. So, I do propose to support each other.

However, if there is any chance that your partner's goal seems to be unrealistic, perhaps it is possible that your support may do more damage than good. In either case, it is your duty to speak on the matter. Be honest and forward, but also take your partner's feelings into consideration. This does not call for one to be rude or callous. Be supportive and caring when addressing the matter, keeping in mind that this is someone's dream or goal, more so your partner's dream, who may have embedded this in him/herself for years, before the two of you became a couple. So, it can be a touchy subject indeed. But always be honest and forthcoming.

Do not just identify where the problem lies, but also offer assistance in terms of how the two of you can come up with a better solution. This approach will be accepted much better. Bringing a solution and not just identifying the problem is always admired. Plus, it is received much better and shows you are interested. The best way to help a partner is to demonstrate support. This is the best way to help one better him/herself, especially when you see things are not successful as they could be. Also remain encouraging when things are on track and going according to plan.

On the flip side, this goes both ways. Both parties should be willing to give advice and support. Now that brings me to the over-persistent mentality I desired to touch on. First, let me say, "over-persistency" or to "impose" on each other when addressing views or ideas belonging to a companion can be damaging. Over-imposing can be a sure way to cause dissention and strife in any relationship, friendship or association of any kind. As adults, we have all been wired a certain way that we are comfortable with, and as some would say, we get stuck in our ways. We all like to be accepted for who we are, not who another desires us to be. Despite religion, political views, the occupation one chooses, or the clothes a person wears, whatever it is, allow him/her the freedom to choose.

Please do not get it confused in any way. I am not saying that it is not good to make suggestions pertaining to the person in question. What I am saying is to go easy on the force. Imposing always extracts the negative out of someone. I am sure we all heard the saying, "You can attract more bees with honey than with vinegar." Well, this can somewhat apply. If there is something you require or something to be accomplished from or through your partner, be polite about it. Do not state it as if you are imposing.

Nobody likes to be dictated to, let alone haggled. In other words, no one likes to be verbally harassed persistently. This will definitely run a person off. In all my years of dealing with family, relationships, and people in general, I have learned how we humans have a tendency of attempting to live vicariously through others, mainly through our partners or family members, with concepts and views favorable to you and unfamiliar to them. That is over-imposing on your behalf, whether acknowledged or not, and this I say is dangerous, because it does not aid in providing a healthy connection. Each and every person in a relationship should always have a choice and should not feel pressured. Communication should always be open and easy. So to everyone who desires a more free-spirited connection, leave all extra imposing and over-persistency mindsets at the door.

Purpose and Self-Love (Establishing)

This idea of love is not just a personal affection we experience with others. Although I briefly touched on it earlier, allow me to go in depth. Naturally, before we can love anyone perfectly, the development of natural and self-love is required, by loving and embracing life and finding purpose. Many individuals seem to lose sight of obtaining happiness, which I believe ultimately is love of life, love of purpose, and love of one's self.

Many people wake up daily and go to sleep every night stuck in a stagnant state of being (mentally or physically). Not living, not enjoying life, and not having a purpose is all contrary to loving oneself. Having a more defined, more profound love demonstrated through actions and deed is conducive to ultimate happiness.

Ask yourself how you would feel if in all your days here on earth, in all your life you never found peace, love for self or happiness, or never established or created anything to be remembered by. Sure, being able to procreate is a gift in itself. However, this is something more personal and definitive than lineage. I am speaking in regards to taking this one chance and opportunity to carve out your space in life. The concept is to find your purpose, to utilize your gift and the abilities you were blessed with, to leave your impression, and to do some good for yourself and others. Some of us naturally understand our gifts and simply just have to scratch the surface and focus, while others must sometimes dig deep into the mind.

Truly, it takes love for self to search out these concepts, all the while demonstrating self-love and loving your purpose. Those who have to dig deep into the mind should know that the brain is a very powerful tool. A talent can be hidden deep and is like an oil well waiting to be tapped. Once it is discovered and exploited, it becomes wealth and energy. It serves a purpose for the good of humanity. My point is that to discover purpose is to discover love, possibly the most gratifying feeling.

Every person desires love, happiness, and purpose, and by all means should strive to achieve it. On a quest for self-love and purpose, I have searched high and low. I have considered many ventures and excursions and made many uncalculated decisions. Some turned out fine, but most turned out to be costly.

Primarily, I was in search of love and purpose, and I foolishly assumed that it could be found in a female companion. However, at the time, I was not mentally stable enough for a companion. I could not give love when I was in search of loving myself and finding purpose. So, there I was searching. I tried the gang life, which was counterproductive and was not for me. I tried selling drugs, also a step backwards. I could not do it. I tried vocation schools, warehouses, jobs, security positions and still no satisfaction. I was searching for something better, something higher, a purpose. I knew that was the only way to fill the void within.

It was my love for self that was driving me. I came to terms with the idea that what I was seeking was a state of consciousness and not anything material. So, I began to search out a purpose to find and utilize my gifts and talents, so I could find happiness within and carve out my space in life to perhaps leave a lasting impression on the world, a legacy. There have been nearly a trillion people who have walked this earth since day one; they came and they went. With a few exceptions, there was no evidence of them ever existing, no historical record, no noticeable contribution, and that bothered me and left me distraught. Therefore, desiring and needing to acquire purpose in my life, I felt it took self-love to dig within to achieve this purpose. To be honest, I am not sure if there is life after this. All I know is life is now, and we all should cherish each breath and maximize every opportunity for a chance at love, purpose, and happiness.

Growing up in a cesspool of drugs, poverty, gangs, and prostitution, I was born at a disadvantage from the start, so I considered any positive achievement or goal accomplished indeed a success achieved against many odds. My point is that regardless of your start in life, it is your duty to strive for greatness. This is your sole responsibility. At any rate, chances must be taken. Always remember those who never took a chance nor ever gave themselves a chance.

Along the way, I started to find pleasure in obtaining knowledge and coming to an understanding of self. By empowering myself with knowledge, I then became able to enrich those I love. Having an impact brought me a sense of purpose and happiness. Now, I do not claim to be a scholar. I, however, have these opinions and thoughts that are unique to me. I found purpose in life, and it was because of self-love and a will to achieve great things. To name the accomplishments is of no importance. What is important here is to inspire creating purpose in life and a self-love within. So, to every male and female who is striving to better your life and conditions, "Reach for the moon with one hand, and reach for the stars with the other."

Personally and professionally, always push forward. Sometimes, we allow small obstacles to hinder our happiness in life. Remain persistent and vigilant, and always give one hundred percent. Anything in life worth having is never easy. Love and happiness are two of the simplest pleasures in life, yet can be war in our attempts to receive them. Again, it always first goes back to self. If you do not love yourself, how can you love somebody else? Find something you love and desire to accomplish, and focus on it. If you have a talent, hone your craft. Do not ignore your blessing. Each and every one of us has a purpose in life.

It is important that we first appreciate life and take advantage of our existence. Development in finding a purpose is indeed a process. It requires energy, maturity, will and desire. Note that will power is significant and is a critical element in achievement in life, and procrastination is the enemy. I am sure we all heard the saying, "Why put off for tomorrow what can be done today?" Trust yourself and know yourself; most importantly, love yourself. Have courage and do not doubt your abilities, no matter what you face.

Every human being at some point faces fear. Whether flying, swimming, love, or public speaking, we all face some type of fear. So, do not feel awkward, different, or alone; it is a normal emotion. I am quoting President Nelson Mandela here: "Courage is not the absence of fear, but the ability to move past it." Acknowledge your fears; face them and move past them.

Briefly, I would like to take a moment and share a tale with all of you: This is a tale of a young boy and a very successful man. The young boy admired the successful man's wisdom, his loving and beautiful wife who adored him, and the high regard that everyone in town professed for him. One day, the young boy positioned himself to meet the successful man while at a lake. Upon meeting, the young boy asked: "Excuse me, sir, but I have a question for you if I may." "Sure," the man said. The boy then asked, "How can I obtain the love, wisdom, and wealth that you so gracefully possess?" The man took the boy's hand and walked into the lake until the water reached the boy's neck, and without warning, the man pushed the boy's head under water holding him there. The boy began struggling trying to come up. The man brought the boy to the surface, and after the boy had caught his breath, the man asked: "When you were under water, what did you desire the most? More than anything in this world'?" The boy replied, "I desired air. I desired to breathe!" The man then said, "When you desire success, love, and wealth as much as you desired to breathe when you were under water, then I will give you the answer you seek. Because then I will know your willingness to achieve is strong and sincere."

The point I'm making is you should desire success as much as you desire to breathe. Therefore, operate without fear. Find your purpose, and search for your happiness. In doing so, you will witness a love and feeling like no other. Do not subject yourself to limitations by any means. Men and women, of all ages and nationalities, you can choose to participate in life. Or, you can do nothing and be a bystander. We all have a responsibility to ourselves and a choice to make a difference. The process of understanding life is to be cherished and enjoyed in every second. Do not let fear of failure prevent you from trying whatever it is you are seeking.

There is a lesson in failed attempts. Primarily, it builds character. Many of the world's greatest men and women, past and present, at one time or another, experienced failed attempts. Rather than conceding, they fought and persevered and that strength of character, that willingness to go relentlessly against the current is what made them great. They never gave up, and they pushed until their mission was completed. They obtained their goal. Success, as with love, has no limits, and life with a purpose is to be conquered. Never stop growing or learning; maximize each and every opportunity.

Create your self-love, and find your purpose in life. Keep your head high and your chin up, no fear and no tears, mind of stone and pushing strong, keeping your will strong like steel. If you do not do it, nobody can do it for you. You are in charge of your life; you are the master. Give your best, and go get it. Do not quit! There are no boundaries for success and no limits.

Life and Purpose

Life is to live, love enjoy and achieve a person's goal,
Life is not to die, hate, enrage and be of disservice to any,
Life is to walk, talk, touch and breathe as with soul.
Life is not to be barred, silent, veiled and perish the unknown
Life is born with sin, which is to be forgiven,
Unbound by any, our minds are freely driven.

As we sleep at night, under the stars, our dreams form,
At sunrise, if we do not act, these dreams are then scorned
To conceive a vision that is beautifully born,
Following your beliefs, you have halfway won.
Life is to live, so achieve and receive,
Life is to live again. Repeat after me.

Better Health and Better Love

Our health plays a major role and function in a relationship. The truth is when both people are healthy, they provide a more joyous and active interaction with one another. Better health means better love. And that leads to more stimulation: mentally, physically and socially. Health primarily dictates our moods in life a lot of times. When we are feeling good about ourselves, it shows and is channeled through our actions. To the man and woman, my only hope is to help create better connections and happier lives. I must admit that I have a passion for seeing happy couples and relationships that are driven by passion, and I am constantly noticing in the news how men and women's health are deteriorating from lack of exercise, unhealthy eating, and unhealthy habits.

However, it is said that health affects behavior and hence relationships, and I know that to be true. Now, most individuals may feel it is only discipline that is required to achieve better health. But, in actuality, it takes personal desire and will power to change. And no, I am not a dream's merchant. My purpose is not to sell you dreams but to interest you in new possibilities, a positive outlook of life, only reality. Despite the joy and pain involved, I am going to keep it real at all costs.

Personally, I have been a smoker for years, and I quit only by will, and I judge no one for his/her decision. Also, I indulge in fast food. I eat sweets and enjoy the tasteful delicacies sophisticated culinary arts have to offer, but always in measure, exercising moderation. I embrace the challenge of moderation and find that exercising it can be a booster in regards to attitude and interaction with my companion and not in a competitive way, more as if it were a shared effort.

To achieve better health does not require one hundred pounds, or anything extreme. I stand at six feet three inches tall and weigh two hundred and forty pounds. However, I am very healthy, have a good heart rate, have good numbers for blood pressure, sugar, and cholesterol, and possess amazing stamina. So, it is not the make or model, but the engine that is under the hood. That refers to how your body runs- if you feel where I am coming from.

Besides, it is rewarding for both parties in the relationship to create and maintain good health because it invites more passion, more interaction, and more intimacy. So, instead of overextending yourself to your jobs, family and careers, take personal time for yourself or with a partner and get the health right. What is twenty minutes a day, four or five days a week? No, this does not require spending money on a gym or attending one, unless that is your choice. Simply, all that is required is will. Exercise can be done in the privacy of one's own domain, and it does not call for anything strenuous, just something to get your heart pumping well and a healthy blood flow.

Choose whatever you feel comfortable with. It is the activity that boosts your endurance, energy and stamina, and on the flip side, it provides you with an improved libido. It is as simple as taking a few minutes of stretching to loosen the body up. Try and find something around the house you can use for light weight lifting. That is if you do not already have dumbbells around the house or perhaps you are located near a Big 5 Sporting Goods, to purchase some. Or, you can improvise, by placing a few books or magazines in a pillowcase to create a type of curling equipment; you know to do strength work, and include some pushups in your routine.

As for aerobics, try jumping jacks, squats, even a few minutes of jogging in place. All are free and can be done at home. Spending twenty minutes doing a few sets a day keeps the heart healthy. I am not a fitness guru. I'm just offering ways to get it started, while saving time and money. All it takes is desire and will to become healthier. It is all for the love of life and love itself.

Also music can be used as a motivator when alone. Even when in another's company, music can help drive you or be an essential element in your routine, Zumba for example. Regardless of your choice, it is your life, and you are free to live how you want. I just would like to see the stimulation enriched. On top of everything, bad health limits one from many possibilities, and most importantly, exercise plays an essential role in lengthening one's life span. It is a fact that longevity is directly related to physical activity. So if not for better health, do it for a better intimate relationship with your partner, and create a better future in the process. You will feel younger and on the bright side of things, your stress levels will lessen and so will your doctor's and prescription bills.

Act now! Do not wait until it is too late. Time waits on no one. Do not be one to regret what can be controlled and changed now. Do not wake up one day finding yourself unhealthy and unhappy, with your love life in the drain and finding it harder to reverse the effects.

So, this brief section is dedicated to all couples and singles, male and female. Again, it is to promote better, active love lives and healthy lifestyles, through discipline. In doing so, you can have love, life and happiness. And you will enjoy the effects. That I promise to each and every person reading this.

Please, do feel me when I say encourage others. If people in your life (family, friend, spouse or companion), whatever their position may be, are making an effort to improve their health, extend mental support. Encourage and push them to keep up their good work, and most often, you will notice physical changes. Then, it is time for well-deserved compliments. Complimenting the person, his/her efforts and hard work is always appreciated and pleasurable to hear, which can also serve as motivation to one's mission. So, encourage each other and compliment one another always. Kind words are always pleasing to the soul. Better health means better love and better life. So, before I end this topic, and sure it was brief, I am hoping it has a positive effect.

So, if you are a person looking to improve your health, all it takes is will and action. Remember, if the chemistry has been limited in your relationship, better health will add to desire and higher libido function. It does not take much to achieve health and happiness. We must want it bad enough, like the tale of the boy and the wise man. I can guarantee you if your relationship is in a rut or stand still from a lack of passion, start practicing exercise together, and you and your partner will notice a change in connecting, passion and activities you share. Do understand that this is just an element amongst many to ignite the chemistry and energy in a relationship, but it is a main factor in a longer healthier, happier life. It is one that we all deserve, which in turn also means less stress.

Fact: Whenever I am under the weather or feeling a bit out of it, I tend to be less happy. On the other hand, when I have been exercising and eating right, my mind and body feel less stressed, stronger, active and happier. Plus factor- I have only had a common cold/flu twice in the past four years. Surely, that comes along with practicing good and strict sanitary habits. Primarily, good health is derived from vitamins and exercise. So, get focused and stay focused. Keep pushing for greatness in health, love, life, and happiness. Better health means better love and life.

Sexual Relations in the Hook-Up Era

Kicking it! Hooking up! One night stands! Marriages! Couples! Open relationships! Everyone, whatever you do or subscribe to, feel me in closing. If you read the first three sections of this book, you have read my opinion concerning a few matters on love, life's purpose, and relation-ships. I do not judge you for your opinion or way of life. However, you will have people in life who are going to hate you for whatever you do. Just keep on being you, the best you can be.

Well, I am sure every human being has one experience in common that we all share and enjoy: sex. I choose to speak on sex and express how the number of STDs, specifically AIDS, are staggeringly high, while destroying communities and families and are growing at a rapid rate. So, I feel it would not be right and it would not be a demonstration of love if I do not address the issue.

This discussion on safe sex is for all sexually active people (singles who are dating or anybody who is not in a monogamous relationship). I find it crazy, with the crucial AIDS epidemic at hand, that people seem more concerned with protection to prevent bearing children than with not contracting AIDS. The concern regarding childbearing comes from both sides: male and female, of not wanting to impregnate or get pregnant. I'm not proud, but I was once blind myself. Right in the process of becoming intimate, I am sure all men have heard the question, "Do you have protection?" And a lot of times sex is not planned, so most likely, "No," is the answer; and in response, the lady requests for the guy to not ejaculate inside of her.

Vice versa, I am sure women have heard a question as well, "Are you protected by birth control?" Rarely is there a concern of contracting a

STD, and truthfully, that is scary. Having a child should be the least concern, with AIDS steadily climbing from ghettos to suburbia.

It should be receiving a disease that makes you pause and ask for protection. Just the thought that one night of passion can issue a death sentence from unprotected sex is scary. Prophylactics are the only way sexually active people can ensure their safety, life and health; and I always like to deal with reality, so to those who are in marriages or in a monogamous relationship: If by any chance you are unfaithful or find yourself in that position, protect yourself. Seriously, I am not saying I condone the behavior, for there is only one judge, and it is not me. But, I am a realist and know that infidelity happens and will always exist. I am saying it will be the most devastating thing to give an STD to a partner who considered the relationship exclusive. So, to anyone and everyone- protect yourself. Regardless of the matter, never judge a book by its cover. Just because it looks good does not always make it good.

To have a platform, it is my duty to help bring change for better, if I'm able. I am hoping all sexually active people feel me from the hood to the suburbs. If this can touch one life, a difference was made, and because AIDS is so prevalent in our lifetime, I felt the need to address the matter that seems to be a plague in my community and many others. Whenever sexually active, protection is showing love and respect for your own life. Start encouraging those in your life who are dear to you to do the same. Truthfully, I believe this is what made me a conscious protective/ committed type. That is another reason why I prefer relationships because I am entrusting my life to that one person, which is why trust and honesty are important. To trust your partner is remaining true.

At any rate, I feel better inside. The sex is more pleasurable, by not having concerns or worries of being sexually infected. So yes, I am a fool for trust and love, along with commitment in my relationship, hoping my partner remains true to me. If not, she should at least have the respect to give me an option to leave or use protection because words cannot express the betrayal and anger I or anyone would feel. AIDS is real and is growing everywhere. My only hope is that we all take heed to these words. If one does not practice abstinence, he/she should keep and use protection. Here is a better one, find that special person to settle down with. To all the sexually active people, get your mind right. The safe way is the only way. Protect first, then enjoy...

Furthermore, sex is to be pleasurable for both men and women. It should always be exciting and always different. Focus on what pleases one another. I do not know if many have witnessed or feel this way, but I believe that sexual intimacy with someone you love is far more satisfying and pleasurable. Whether it is a quickie or a marathon session, it is always great. It seems almost 90% of the time that you understand each other's bodies better. Healthy active sex lives create durability in relationships, setting you up for the stretch. I am sure it is universal and equally desired to have a partner with a healthy libido and who enjoys pleasing you. Do not be afraid to try new things, such as different positions, and no matter what, always keep foreplay incorporated.

In all sessions of lovemaking, whether it is passionate and slow or rough and quick, let the foreplay set it up. For couples, just because the relationship has grown or evolved to more, do not stop the excitement. Continue to explore; change up the scenery. Try renting a room at a hotel for the weekend. Go rent a cabin in the mountains or in the snow, without it being a special occasion, just to ignite passion, keeping things heated between you and your partner. Remember, sex is mental just as much as it is physical. So, don't be shy to communicate anything: desires, fantasies, and positions. Express it all.

In the event of having sex or not at the moment, if you are expressing yourself about sex, your request is being heard, and it is welcome. It is natural for us to be in tune and receptive when requests are made to likes and dislikes, and disregard the negative people's attitude towards sex.

Sex is not a bad thing and should not be looked at in such a bad way. It is a way of life that is natural and normal. Sex is more relevant to life than many things. It is able to bring lives together, along with creating life! That is powerful. I think society paints too many negative portraits of sex. Sex sometimes can be used as a tool of power. Say a person applies for a job and regardless of being more qualified, sex can alter the choice. Sex has been known to be used for manipulation, for or to do something. Even though this is deemed bad, it is right. The power of sex will always exist. It is out of anyone's control.

This is a major part of life, and you will find that many do not get it regularly and would like to, just like there are many who do get it regularly and are 'very' glad they do. Sex is on TV, in movies, on the Internet, on street corners, magazines, novels, you name it. Humans are sexual beings, and that will never change. But before I turn the corner, to everyone- learn how to discover love. Sex is not love. Sex is sex, and knowing the difference will save a lot of broken hearts.

People confuse sex with love all the time, and just because intimacy is occurring or has occurred, do not think love is to follow. I spoke earlier on how to create love. Now, one must know it and receive it. It is not from a womb or a penis; I assure you that. Sex is a real pleasure and can be ecstasy. However, it can create temporary feelings, sometimes both, physical and mental, and it definitely creates lust, and a lot of times, the two can be confusing from the beginning. The two are lust and love. Both deal with passion, affection and desire for each other. However, lust is not mutual. It has no foundation, and there is no mental component. Lust does not require knowing or understanding the person. It is brief and is subject to change for any reason; whereas, love is the complete opposite.

First and foremost, you will know it is love because your desires, feelings, and concerns would be reciprocated. Love is making an effort to know and understand you- anything and everything about you, present, past and future. So even though you are enjoying the sex, do not confuse it. Know the difference between lust and love when sex is involved. The crazy thing is love can occur at any moment. But if you are having sex before the love is there, it really makes it difficult to determine the emotions that are being felt at that time. I have come to know a lot of people who claim they share a love. But when asked they do not know anything about the person they are with, but they call it love.

The fact is- I do not find it crazy because I know how powerful sex can be. Sex has the power to make you think a certain way, act differently, and say things incoherently. So, personally I try to follow my heart, and advise all to take your time with love, just to be sure. Because the reality is no person desires to be misled or heartbroken due to misjudgment. It is good to err on the side of caution if hearing, 'I love you,' for the first time right after sex. Love is love.

All in all, enjoy life, love, and passion. There is nothing wrong with having a healthy sex life. Just take notice in the times we now live in. Practice safe sex. Protection first, then enjoyment. If you are going to do it, do it right. Respect yourself, and love your life. I am not preaching or lecturing. I only tell you because I care. Do not let twenty minutes of passion cause you a lifetime of pain.

PART FOUR

K. Antwon Buckner

Love Unmeasured

My love for you can never be measured.
And in the depths of my heart you will always be treasured.

This love for you is different by far,
Full time for life, true to the end from the start.

You're the air I breathe, the ground that supports me, my earth underneath ...

My love for you will be recognized deeper than fame,
My concern, love and passion for you burns like hot flames

Sex ain't never better than love.
You complete me as heaven sent from above.

Trust is what we share and always consider it sublime,
Like the sun in the sky that is destined to shine.

Some things are unexplainable, like who we love or is it true,
So we let our actions reveal along with time when it's due.

It takes two to be involved, a connection deeper than sex.
Two minds and two souls moving as one with no regrets.

You're beautiful sunshine not just in face but in mind,
It's your essence, presence, and intellect that adds to your shine.

I will cherish you daily, keeping my memories at heart -
Letting nothing come between us to the end from the start.

Sincerely, I am in Love with You

It's hard to describe how I feel for you in words,
And even harder to show being I'm caged up like a bird.
I pray we don't clip our wings before our chance to fly away.
My strength and vision is to love you, with no other filling that space.
Sincerely in love.

In the midst of any troubles, plights are the test.
I hope our love overpowers to help us see our success.
When I think of love and destiny, it's you that tugs on my chest.
I'm wishing to stay in your life, fight for you, and give you my best.
Please stay present in my life, connected and steady.
So know the thought of us not together breaks my heart already.
Sincerely in love.

Strive and Sacrifice

As I strive for the best and push hard to achieve,
Got me calculating each step
Due to the pressure life brings.

Like a soldier at war, I adapt to survive -
Remaining strong by all means.
Staying focused and wide-eyed.
Trust is always a factor in which I live and learn.
People with masks and fraudulent ways
Make it hard to discern.

There is no pleasure in pain,
There is no glory in vain.
More animalistic than you think,
But I'm trying to stay civil and sane.

Like scattered stars across the sky,
Potential of temptation rates are high.
I'm constantly struggling to live when
We're living to die.

But all in all, it's my life, and I'm a do as I please,
Still laying my dreams by the wayside
To help my people in need.
Sure, we all die alone, but it's together we breathe...

Under the Stars

Strong affectionate kisses we exchange under the stars.
Our eyes shut and tongues touch and
The moon becomes ours.
As we passionately embrace, bringing our bodies as one,
Shared in the chill of night our physical remains warm.
The taste of your love I aim to achieve;
The pleasure is mine as
Your essence weakens my knees.
Injecting myself into your anatomy and soul.
With a most sincere heart I'm about to lose all control.
I engage with a force, turning a spark to a flame.
It was a beautiful dark night, but
Now the sunshine came.
Long affectionate kisses under the stars we exchange.

K. Antwon Buckner

Misled and Abandoned

With a kiss, you said you love me,
But you're not at my side by choice.
We encountered under the stars at night -
Perhaps, it was to the sound of my voice.

Could it have been my poetic connotations
That briefly enraptured you about?
The truth about life is that sparks burn out;
I consider ours a flame that would burn, no doubt.

You misled and abandoned me, and
Served cuts to the chest;
In the midst of my troubles, my plight and my test,
Not knowing the depths of my struggles will determine
The height of my success.

The thing that sustains me is
I am a pillar of strength.
I no longer think of your false love.
That was dealt with remiss,
And I've buried those memories
And sealed the end with a kiss.

Ultimate Unknown

Accompany me if you're looking for the
Ultimate leap into the unknown. Where nights
Are cold, hearts are below zero, and children force
To be grown. I welcome you, leap into the ultimate unknown.
Young girls abused, used and pregnant at 15,
Uneducated, no support of any means, no goals and no
Dreams. It's even worse for young boys; they hit prison
By 14, and his mother's lost her job. Now he feels
Compelled by any means. With only two choices, Robin
Hood or the drug scene. Oh, did I forget to mention he is
A daddy to be, that's another mouth to feed -from that
Abused pregnant girl that is 15, put yourself in their
Shoes, where the slums are their thrones. I welcome you
To leap into the ultimate unknown.

Outside looking in, you can't see the damage that unfolds;
Some wounds may be visible, but the majority
Psychologically shown. Often questioning humanity, lost
Religion through despair, where the sun never shines,
Wondering why no one cares.

I care and submerge myself as part of the unknown,
Changing rooks to queens and turning pawns into kings.
Paving roads of gold and making grass become green,
Once was ghetto slums, now paradise to behold. Look
How I leaped to change the ultimate unknown.

I'll Never Change

My opinions are mine, my views I believe,
Making my own path, so please don't impede.
Costly mistakes on the way,
I didn't give up and didn't concede.

Learned from experience, not teachers
Or universities. Every step I found hard
But brought me close to my goal.

Broken promises and let downs left so many scars, so I
Don't trust nobody, word to the moon and the stars.

Work hard for what I want,
Stayed focused and on guard;
Sacrifices came with a push forward,
I am in charge.

Some days I am a gentleman and hood the next;
Other days I am simpler than the next
Complex. Mind of a philanthropist, C.E.O., or tyrant,
Depending on what you make me, that's what you get.

Real with those who are real with me and
One thing shall remain, "I'll never change me."

Sharing Your Love

Can you vision sharing your love,
With a man locked in a cell?
With no intentions of judging him and
Letting time reveal.
Intrigued by his knowledge, intellect, and his skills,
Followed by passion and romance, honesty and sex appeal.
Foundation of early stages, developed by will,
No longer hesitant, now you're looking forward to build.
Never envisioned your love being sent from a cell,
He always brings out the best in you.
Finally a man you can feel. Support and love
Remains mutual, he always passes your tests.
The rewards of not judging created a friendship
That's deep. That being the foundation, constructed a love
That is complete. Until he's released, his only request is
Persevere through lonely nights, strive and give it your best.

K. Antwon Buckner

Speaking to the Soul

Picture having the ability to make a heart rush,
Making a mind race, create a blush without touch.

Bubble baths for two, and sharing walks on the beach.
Candle lights or fireplace, a true passion that's deep.

From the moment of blush, dialogue was shared
With no speech, something stronger than pride,
The art to talk and not speak.

Body language is dialogue, this is far more advanced,
No signs, no words, many think it's a trance.

I'll share with you one time, and try to go slow,
Focused attention is needed,
Conveyed thoughts is the goal.

Most think eye contact is a game, of who
Holds and who folds. On the contrary, it's a connection
Entering the window of the soul.

Eyes are the windows to the soul
So to open the window is the ultimate goal.
And the message that's told is spoken soul to soul.

More Than Words

There is nothing more in unison,
Than how you extend when I reach.
No words are exchanged
Learning your body as you teach.
You captivate my mind; it's through
The heart we do speak.

Our minds are in sync,
Hearing each other's thoughts when we think.
Surrender ourselves as complete
Communicating without speech.
Like a gaze at the sunset,
That I find beautiful and amazing.
Your love is truth to the soul
That I will cherish each day.

Leaders

When followers become leaders,
Their position is noticeably changed;
Their actions remain bold,
Though their mindset is why they reign

Refusing to succumb to the toils of another,
Blazing their own path unbound by any other.

Every day their prayer is to strengthen minds,
Body, and soul, soul being eternal,
Body for present, mind so one doesn't fold.

On a journey where wisdom can't be bought,
Only bestowed, never speak of one's deeds,
Demo their actions by show.

Striving for success accomplishing goal after goal
Leaders create landmarks, follower quid pro quo.

Remarkable

Our love is remarkable, forever we shine,
Standing stronger than pride, forever you're mine.
I got you, my love; we are destined to be.
When thinking of what beauty is, it's your face that I see.

Just the thought of your smile,
I grin and yearn for your touch,
My mind starts racing
Bringing my heart to a rush.

A beautiful love that stands against all odds, like cold
Winter night, followed by sunny blue skies.

I'm not concerned about other people, or what's on their minds,
In you, I found a soul mate, bringing joy for a lifetime.
I've seen many men cry, as sure as white doves fly,
But I've never seen a love so remarkable as you and I.

Just Wanna See You Smile

Excuse me beautiful,
Why are you looking so hostile?
I only spoke to get acquainted, and
Noticed a bruise when you profiled.
You say love's making you stay,
But look at your beautiful face.
I'm making it my business, and
I am probably out of place, but why stay
If he beats on you, as if there is no other way?

And just a quick heads up, it's not love why you stay,
Love is given with smiles, not fists in the face.
So if you wanna get away, make a choice here today -
Real love does exist, but you're going the wrong way.

I can tell you how to get there and
What to look for if you like,
It's all love, support, and kindness,
No abuse, no strife; loyalty, passion,
Respect, no harm, no fools.
There's no need to say thank you,
I just wanna see you smile.

I Miss You

I miss you my dear,
Like a night without stars.
Sure, the moon's still there,
But it's the stars we call ours.
Like late night without sleep, or
Deep sleep without dream -
Days without your presence,
I can't justify the means.
I need you here, there is no room
For my heart to grow fonder.
Each moment without you
Makes my heart pound thunder.
Like dark cloudy days, where the sun
Seeps through the seams -
Those days you are missed most,
If you know what I mean.
Physically and mentally trust it gets hard.
I miss you my dear, like a night without stars.

Journey

Journey with me to the land of love,
No interruptions, no phone calls,
Just passion and us.
No inhibitions, no drugs,
The ecstasy we are going for doesn't come in a pill.
Don't be afraid, I got skills, so relax and
Just chill, I know you're used to the fake,
But now witness the real.

Journey with me to the land of love,
Where our fantasies become reality.
If you are afraid to go, let me know now,
Once this ride takes off it's not slowing down.
Soft caress that's nice, strawberries and ice,
Take my time with your body, so I know it's done right.

Journey with me to the land of love.
Touching parts of your body you never knew existed,
Causing pain and pleasure, from my tongue
To your lips. Don't cover your eyes
There's no need to be ashamed.
But after tonight, bet the neighbors know my name.

Believe

Please believe in our love and consider it divine.
Like the sun and the moon that are destined to shine.

Please believe in our friendship, and
Know there is nothing I would change.
Honesty, support, loyalty and commitment
Shall always remain.

Please believe in our companionship, romance, and
Passion by all means. Supportive of each other and
Achieving our dreams as a team.

Please believe in our marriage, the pain and
Joy we both share. Vowing for a lifetime,
Embracing our journey with no fear.

Please believe in our future, and
The next lifetime that follows.
Cherishing today's moments and
Looking forward to tomorrow,
Remaining soul mates in this life,
The next, and one that follows.

K. Antwon Buckner

Your Letter

I received your letter today and I
Must say it drove me wild.
I read it more than ten times and
Every time I smiled.

Considering every sentence,
Clinging to every word -
I even kissed the paper,
I know it may sound absurd.

But emotions run high,
Especially since we are apart.
Producing feelings of need
With an open mind and heart.

When separated by distance,
I feel a pain in my chest.
When spending time and bonding,
In those times I feel blessed.

You are a force in my life and
I am glad we are together.
I pray our love never changes and
Remains constant and forever.

Only For You

Only for you am I driven to poetically write.
I may be aggressive, but that's
Love and emotions, compelling me to recite
From your invite.

We're so connected that I feel you in your silence;
You inspire me as one like a motivational speaker.
Delivering profound as a professor, patience of a teacher.

Only for you am I driven to poetically write.
With thoughts of your smile, I stand in awe saying, "Wow."
Hoping to learn your mind more intimately,
Releasing seeds after I plow.

Attentive and protecting you,
Vowing to bond with you I pledge.
When you need anything, before you ask,
Know I'm two steps ahead.

Only for you.

It's You

Here I am, a grown man, and you make me
Feel the butterflies of a teenager in love.
Nobody is promised the next minute of
Breath, so I cherish every moment and
Consider every thought of you, and now
Understand the true meaning of life.

A love that's shared spiritually first and foremost.
No material or amount of money can ever compare.
You make me dream at
Day, and sleep peaceful at night. I'm human
So yes it hurts to see you hurt. It pains
Me to know you pain. I'm overjoyed when
You're happy, and I smile when you are
Relaxed and at peace: mind, body, and soul.

What is this? When I can't hear your voice
Its' unbearable agony. To think of a life
Without the softest kisses from you is
Torture. All you have to do is exist
And I'll love you with action. The concept
Of this is deep. You push me to try
Hard and don't know it. Commitment
Has been a thought, but you make me
Practice it, and do not know it.

It's you.

All In

From the first day we met,
Your face I knew I would not forget.
No matter how painful or joyous
It is, there are no regrets.

You won my heart, and our souls
Are intertwined by design.
No matter where we are in this
Life, forever you're mine, so shine.

I gave you my heart, not to be abused
But used, in a good way all day.
When you wish for me to go,
My heart and soul shall stay, together we
Stand -I always remain.

Who you give your love to is not
Only a question. And when I ask you
To sacrifice, it's more than a suggestion.
Words mean nothing, forever I will
Display my expression.

Blue Tears

Not to confuse them with fear, but
These tears are from pain. Fell in
Love with the blue team, and ever since
It's been rain.

This blue is unbreakable- even harder to
Shake, it offers only a little while
Demanding more on the take.
Pledging my life to the blue- in vain
Destroying a dream. Drug sales, robberies,
Death and destruction it brings.

In the depths of my mind, I struggle to change.
Constant heartaches, wishing for rain.

Not to confuse them with fear, but
These tears are from pain.

The one that was once true, cannot can't be trusted
It seems. Tear drops that are blue, from fake
Friends that deceive.

Cloudy days trump sunshine, many years in
Darkness. Observing one living in those caves,
While thinking on souls in the graves. Nightmares
And migraines, frustrations and pains. See it clearly
Now; beautiful mind trapped in the shade. Now pushing
For better, I strive for change. "Must stay true." But
When the stress gets too painful, my teardrops come in blue.

Make It

Every step that's made,
Every breath that's took;
Every choice we make and
Every place we look,
should be for better.
A better self, life, and love. And that's
My push. I don't do it for just me. But
For all those who are active in my life.
I push for us both. When it's too tough,
Call on me, where I will stand firm with
You. But in this life, most say it's a game
To be played. So if you're reading this note:

Knowledge is power- but only when used
Correctly. Potential is cool, but without
Performance, it's nothing. Respect is never
Given, it's demanded. If you can envision it,
You can get it. Never doubt oneself if
The first attempt fails. Reflect,
Analyze, and correct, then try again.
Winning is not everything.
It's the only thing.
Ain't no limit to success.
"If you want it, go get it."

Expressed

This gift of ours that we call life is
Much bigger than an image or mere words.
I speak truth some may find absurd.

Just because I associate with you, don't
Confuse it as though you're part of my
Sphere. Fair warning, no fear.
I remain meticulous about those I
Allow in my realm. Many say life's a
Movie, but I assure- you can't rewind the film.

Not ego-trippin', just expressing my
Movement. In the circle of Society, the only
Variety, we seek other than wealth and peace.
Is loyalty, devotion, respect, reliance, and
Strength. Mind of a scholar, heart of a beast.

A bond that gets broken is a bond that
Never was. In honor, we commit. Either we're
In or we're out. No half stepping meaning, no
Doubts. When things come to an end, it at
Many times remains just that. It's okay to look
Back sometimes, but never do we move backwards!

We all have our own plights, philosophy and views.
Some can relate, many left confused. As humans, we
Evolve, so if being one way is considered real,
Consider me not. I've many layers and change
Accordingly. You get what you bring out of me.

Remember Me

If I die before my time, let those
That ask know that I was a warrior.
Stood tall and always strove
For greatness.
Loyalty makes you family- not
Blood. In all my efforts to obtain,
Wealth was and is for the betterment
Of my friends and family. Never for
Self-enjoyment, it's for consoling those in my life.
"Remember Me."

Never had a problem to carry the
Weight and burdens of all mine, I ride
And rode with no hesitation. In trepidation...
If needed, I went and got it, for myself
And you all, without stall.
When I was called upon, I stood up and
Stood firm "Remember Me"

Made mistakes, and learned lessons,
Many hurt, but made me smarter and
Stronger, appreciating blessings...
With hands tied, I did, do, and can
Make mountains move.
Only by faith and works, hard efforts
Were made to look smooth.
"Remember Me"

Always exerted respect, passion, courage, and
Strength, attitude, savvy, discipline, and
Ambition within... "Remember Me"

Hard Days & Rough Nights

As I struggle in this world designed for all of humanity
Living is easy for some, but I'm fighting ways of insanity.
Life is a quest full of trials and full of tests,
On a journey with no friends and no guests,
And a mind with no rest.

As for the test- I'm prepared,
As for no friends- I don't care,
As for the mind with no rest,
Now the problem lies there,
While I'm searching for my fortune,
I have dreams of peace and
Changed ways.

Hoping to one day live righteous, and
Finally see better days.
Swear to die on my feet than live a life on my knees.

I was working a week ago,
But the company is now overseas.
No food and I'm hungry, rent's due and
I'm broke, my community already broken,
I'll hurt them more selling dope.
Robbery's no option; it's not worth the result,
Let me share how it goes -
Not including the charge and
The strife the courts will dig up,
The gun is ten off the top,
And that is messed up.
So that's thirty-four years gone for a few hundred bucks,
These are choices and the life that I led

With everything looking hopeless yet, and still I believe.
Stuck between a rock and a hard spot,
Which way should I lean?

Love the Way You Love

I love the way you love,
Because it's not complicated.
I got a big ego, and never are you intimidated.
Loyalty and honesty, your love is brand new
I love the way you love me, so giving and so true.

Your tasty lips to kiss and sweet hugs to hold.
I appreciate your touch and much more, truth be told.
I love the way you love and, for the record, seven fold.

Ghetto Proverbs

Life offers a vicious cycle of ups and downs.
Success entices us with luxuries and
Beautiful women to show around.

Like parachute in use, the mind is dared to stay open,
Decipher the pros and cons of advice that is spoken;
Learn from mistakes; they should never be repeated;
"Where there is a will, there is a way."
Never accept being defeated.

Be thankful for your life, a gift it truly is;
That's why it's called the present -
For the time in which we live.

On a mission of success, watch your enemies
And keep friends closer. Finish all of what you start and
Bring all affairs to closure.

Disappointed

You said you'd lift me up!
If I ever were to fall!
But you disappointed me!
Cause when times got rough,
You didn't stand tall!
It's easy when speaking on things you're going to do
But those are just words
Without the action it ain't true
Had me sitting here waiting on you
Time and time again
But you left me disappointed
By flaking on me in the end!
Now, I'm scratching my head wondering
What's the point of a friend?
When I call it disappointment,
You call it love that you send.

I Stand With You

Through the fame, through the fire and
The flames, you intoxicate my brain and
I adapt to the pain. Be clear that the
Streets are a strain! And when it
Rains, it rains.

I was once in this alone,
But now it's you I call my own.
It's always a pleasure, whenever we collide,
Walking in this cold world, just you and I.
Like ancient soldiers of Rome,
We war to protect our throne.
Through the high valleys and low deserts, swamps to the North Pole.
Constantly, we stand as one,
Praying to never fold truth be told.
Nobody knows where we will be,
So I'm injected into your soul.
That way I'm always with you
No matter where we are to go...

Materialized Dream

It's our love that I see hidden in the shadows of my mind,
Though I struggle like one grasping for a hummingbird, or better yet,
A butterfly beautiful, captivating and hard to catch.
All while in the realms of my mind,
It seems as if you're sunken to the depths of my cerebral,
But the thoughts of you trigger emotions to the heart
As though I have you in my arms to hug, hold, and caress.
A tear of joy is shed because it feels good to finally touch you
And see the beautiful face that was hid in the shadows of my mind.
Am I dreaming?
Or has that beautiful, captivating, hard to catch source finally materialized?
Truly it's a moment I choose to cherish for life,
So if I'm dreaming, don't wake me.
If not, these mind formations are truly what dreams are made of...

Visionary

As with all things in life, greatness comes with great sacrifice,
And before obtaining greatness, we sometimes take many small losses.
It's like fighting many battles before winning the war,
And sometimes those battles can be dominant enough to stop you
From fighting and disrupting your focus, creating a negative force by
Stopping your drive and ambition,
Leaving you to only imagine what could have been, only to think of the victory.
Most think having a vision or being a visionary is to be special and unique.
On the contrary, it takes determination.
There is no greater feeling in life than to have a successful accomplishment,
To start something important to you, and regardless of the challenges, complete it.
Indeed, it brings a most elated feeling and creates a feeling of empowerment,
Directed towards your will, mind state, and aura.

Companion for Me

I don't desire a super model, but a companion.
I don't need a person looking to be completed,
But a person who's already comp1ete,
A companion that will have my back,
Yet stand and remain at my side.
There's no need for her to constantly profess how sweet,
How caring, how attentive, and loving she is,
Because in the darkest hour,
Those characteristics shine bright with no question.
Being able to form one's own opinion and the understanding
To acknowledge validity, and courage to change that opinion,
Showing humility. A companion that doesn't run from these faults
But recognizes and embraces them and vows to change those faults.
And lastly, how's her love in ways pleasant and agreeable to her...

My Voice

It's strange how pain can weigh heavily on the heart..
Thoughts that concern me still, where do I start
In a world so cold, where words are just trends;
Why bite my tongue for posers and fake friends?

Politicians are the same, cutting programs of helping hands,
And have the audacity during ballot season to preach, "United we stand."

Family is supposed to be your backbone, which is few if proved true;
I find more opposition from within than I do from you,
So forgive me if I don't align or mingle well at times.

In a world that is so cold, perhaps I've been infected with its design.
Just a few of my thoughts and concerns and the pain in my heart.

Now, if I only had a voice.
Where do I start?

My Love Is

My love doesn't change from situation to situation,
Because my love is much deeper than a wavering emotion.
My love is conscious my choice to share my responsibility.
My desire and effort to be a part of something much bigger
And more beautiful than my single imperfect self.
My love is understanding, forgiving, and enduring
Because in love, all I ask is to be understood and accepted.
My love is the result of and reward in the embrace, connection,
And commitment of two souls.
The promise and comfort of knowing in nothing you stand alone.
My love, even in all of its imperfections, is meant to build,
Make whole, to provide for and to protect the heart, mind and soul.
My love is vulnerable and warm, giving and strong.
My love is the core of who I am,
The tie that binds my sanity and defines my purpose as a man.
And it's a blessing to have you in my life,
Because my love is you!

Time After Time

It's you that I call on when all else fails,
'Cause I know you won't let me down and
You've always been there.

Time after time, you come through.
There is no mistaking -you care.
Well, this request is a bit different,
With effect of changing your life
My wish is to be there for you;
Not in part, but full time.
I'm thinking of ways to propose,
Hearing wedding bells and sharing vows.
Before you call, I'm already there,
Placing your needs before mine, and
No need to look for, always right by your side.
You will never have to wait. I'll be there in the dime,
My love is forever, time after time.

Ecstasy For Two

I'm glad you love the way I kiss and
Find comfort in my hold.
I love your eyes and lips, and
Find comfort in those.
Exchanging intimate knowledge
What you expect to be shown.
To witness the pleasure you seek,
Just take my hand and let's go.
With the mood being just right,
You feel it's time that we grow.
Welcome to intimate ecstasy and
Ladies first, so you know.
And if I'm moving too fast,
Just say the word so I know.
While saying the pace is just right,
You're shaking, losing control.
Ecstasy for two, time of arrival the same,
I'm glad I was invited, and
Even more that you came.

Love of Your Own

Nothing can compare to a love of your own.
I wish to be king, and you the queen to my throne.
You offered your heart and your love for the taking,
I promise the same, and it will not be forsaken.
Sometimes, my emotions I cannot control,
These words that I speak are truth to the soul,
Nothing can compare to a love of your own.

K. Antwon Buckner

Ways of a King

Prepare myself for war in my attempts to be supreme.
Master of my temptations,
Seeking my place amongst kings.
When faced with afflictions
I persevere by all means.
Unbound by tribulations,
I am in control as in my dreams.
Call it a war cry, a threat, or a song,
Just be sure to prepare for my coming and
Polish up my throne.

Forever and Again

Your love and honesty is far special and unique,
One that I do appreciate,
No other companion or me.

To point out the reasons is necessary indeed,
Trust and embrace this experience that is destined to be.

I am loving your eyes, hips, lips, and your thighs,
Beautiful smile and a cute face, you're humble with grace.

These desirable thoughts of you can go on without end,
Just as my love shall endure for you forever and again.

Hope It's You

Hope it's you!
Someone who can satisfy my every lil' need
I'm hopin' it's you
I've been waitin' for someone to bring her love to me
Wonder if you're qualified to give me love and affection
In my mind girl, I'm hoping it's you
Cause things neva seem to go my way
I've been hurt sooo many times before
And I need a lil' something more
I'm hopin' it's you
There's plenty opportunity if you want to be my lady
I want you to know that people say I'm hard to please
So come and change my world
Put your heart into it
And everything will be alright
You got to promise to be that special woman in my life
I'm hopin' it's you!

Satisfaction

You have the ability to make my mind race.
You captivate my heart, with the trace of every space.
Conscience or unconscious, I think of you before myself.
I strive for better in life to ensure I better yours.
My endearment reigns high as the mountaintop.
My love for you contains no expectations.
I'm protective of you and defend with no intimidation.
I place myself in harm's way to remove you from it.
I won't hesitate to give all when called upon it.
My loyalty remains unconditional and constant indeed.
My joy is found pleasing you.
My fascination is how I'm drawn to your soul with every effort.
I stand firm and unwaivering.
No question, yes I'm satisfied.
With a taste, I'm savoring...

I'll Never Change

My opinions are mine, my views I believe,
Making my own path, so please don't impede.
Costly mistakes on the way,
I didn't give up and didn't concede.

Learned from experience, not teachers
Or universities. Every step I found hard
But brought me close to my goal.

Broken promises and let downs left so many scars, so I
Don't trust nobody, word to the moon and the stars.

Work hard for what I want,
Stayed focused and on guard;
Sacrifices came with a push forward,
I am in charge.

Some days I am a gentleman and hood the next;
Other days I am simpler than the next
Complex mind of a philanthropist, C.E.O., or tyrant,
Depending on what you make me, that's what you get.

Real with those who are real with me and
One thing shall remain, "I'll never change me."

Tempting

Such an alluring presence
Whose glow is felt by the warmth it produces
Being fully cast in its shine is here man
Wants to thrive in
Like forbidden fruit
A lil' taste of mouthwatering temptation
Is all that's needed.
Tempting isn't it?
To have something so good
So close yet so far
That you can smell the sweetness and imagine the juiciness
If ever you were to have just one bite
Tempting isn't it?
To be led astray by the many distractions and crave the many flavors
That surrounds you daily
Only to know you can get burnt if you were to touch the untouchable
Why is life so tempting?

Intelligent

Mental stimulation
Now I'm full,
Off food for thought.
A knowledgeable investigation
Using the lesson I was taught.
Intelligence is captivating
When pole vaulting a mindset and
Navigating around hurdles.
Mentally reaching for my place.
A beautiful face
For the cameras.
Though over time it's bound to change
An intelligent intelligence only
Magnifies the brain
So every book you choose to read
And report you choose to write,
Will enhance your education cause it's needed in this life.

Let Live

It's a thin line.
Yet there's a big difference in living for something and dying for nothing.
One of which there is no return from.
So, let your choice and belief in the decision be made with wisdom and understanding.
Love, Family, and Liberty are always worth a sacrifice to breathe for.

Love's Essence

Only I know the instinctive movements you make in my dreams.
As I reach for you only to chase a shadow, softly, softly you go away.
Awaking late nights at the edge of loneliness, no one in my corner.
Yet, thoughts of being with you quiet my soul.
If only to have you in life as I do in my dreams I say wait just a while.
Don't move for now, not yet.
After every dream when I awake, I ask myself what's the meaning.
I hope that wasn't the last occurrence.
Thoughts drift and silence sets for a moment.
Imagining quick soft kisses and a warm touch.
Smelling your scent from letters and pics thinking, …
So, I force myself back to sleep, just to feel your touch…

Can You Imagine

Imagine
Having passionate sex in a hot air balloon
You wanted a present? Here's the moon.
Imagine
A romantic candlelight dinner on the pier slow dancing.
Holding you tight whispering in your ear.
Imagine
A poetic scenery of rolling greens along a plain!
Walking hand in hand
Sharing our goals and dreams
Imagine
Being at the beach,
On a blanket sipping wine.
Watching a view of the sunshine decline.
Telling jokes causing laughter…
Imagine

Happy Anniversary

I know this lady
Who's so special to me
It drives me crazy
Today's our anniversary
It's just her and me
Against all odds
While conquering temptations that Satan brings
She makes my heart sing
She is my everything
A true friend indeed
Is what I need
I'm overjoyed with how she reveals herself to me
Thank you
For everything you've done
Been an angel since day one
And blessed me
This is my dedication
To bring a smile upon your face
Along with my loving tender care and warm embrace
Miss you girl
Happy Anniversary!

My Jewel

I adore you through pleasure and pain,
Forever my queen, so together we reign.
Excuse my stress or the times I'm upset.
But in pain I still love aiming to give you my best.
So, I hope you take solace in knowing you make me feel blessed.
Your beautiful eyes, smile and lips to match.
And those thighs my goodness YAH know He did that.
You're a jewel, and I know it.
Indeed a pleasure to grow with.
I love the way you love me even when you try not to show it.
My jealously is bad, read this again and you'll understand why.
Cause you're a jewel and my queen.
Brightest star to light the sky.

Holidays

Holidays, Holidays, Holidays, oh how I've waited all year for you!
To see the white snowcaps decorating the mountaintops
To see the fresh prints of rabbits and deer in the snow
To decorate and customize the Christmas tree
All year long, I've waited for this day, so I can be free to do me
To visit family I only get to see for the holidays
To finally appreciate the warmth of a fireplace and not the heater
The one day you can kiss multiple women without being called a cheater
Holidays, Holidays, Holidays, oh how I've waited all year for you!
To sip on a cup of hot cocoa with lil' marshmallows in it
To partake in the excitement of lighting up the house with Christmas lights
To be old fashioned for at least one day and buy one another a gift to show your
appreciation
To enjoy the smiles you're able to place on a loved one's face despite what he/she may
be going through
The best day to lose yourself in the magic of carolers
To go to church and celebrate Christ's birth
Holidays, Holidays, Holidays, oh how I wait all year for you!

Clearly

Out of nowhere here we meet
It's like the clouds moved out the way to show this Star........
I'm in your life to stay and now you feel it's natural to not go far,
Dedicated to this foundation, I need more than a bar...
Most people feel you'll vanish in the 1ˢᵗ storm,
Not aware something strong was born, when our friendship was formed...
Blessed by the Most High, our souls can't be torn, weathering any storm, not vowing,
Not sworn, via magnetic born, invisibly worn, from where our energy's drown.
You love it when I kiss you, with a touch that's miss able,
With passion that's attestable,
It's only Me and You
So the screaming glory is acceptable,
Along with expected though .....

Hold on Tight

If you give me your hand, I promise to hold on tight,
If you need me to sing, I'll offer a melody that'll
Soothe you through the night ...
Believe and Achieve, Commit not Stray ....
It's good to materialize Dreams so Hope and Pray
Life at times may get hectic, when journeying.
Along this path but let prayer be your helmet,
Knee and Elbow Pads ...
I will never say hold you down,
Cause my Aim is building You Up,
In your defense, I'll act as a Volcano, Diplomatic Primarily
Yet with ease I Erupt.
I'm not at all perfect, a mistake or two I might make
It's the flaws that help me see the beauty we create,
How you fit into my life, encouraging me to be great ...
You will feel my appreciation and respect, not once thinking twice...
Acknowledging your Intellect and Qualities, to Love You is a Delight ...
If You Give Me Your Hand, I Promise To Hold On Tight...

BETRAYAL

Why the hell did I trust you,
Is what I ask myself daily.
The smile that you showed me
Was one of deceit so shady.
BETRAYAL....
You fooled me no doubt
Thought game recognized game
Learned the hard way, you wasn't about the life
You claimed, when you whispered my name.
BETRAYAL...
You were a weed that strangled the life out of a
Beautiful flower before it grew.
Only if you knew!
BETRAYAL...

K. Antwon Buckner

It's Incumbent

We all possess Talents and Strengths,
Rather hidden or found ... When discovered we hone it
Considering it Profound....
Few of mine sharing to motivate, to persevere
When times are tough, able to conceive,
Believe and Achieve and Overcoming when times rough...
Seeking one's victory in all battles,
Theory and form is a must
Having my name placed amongst great men,
Far beyond exposing a Diamond in the rough.
I'm amused you assume I desire jewels, women, prestige or fame.
Suffice it to say it's wealth that's Strength.
A State of being like the legacy of a King.

My Kinda Love

"My Kinda Love is like no other."
Search throughout the Land and the Planet
No one comes close; you can't understand it.
Kind words with actions to follow.
Every deed full of love, not one left Hollow.
Sacrifice with no hesitation, Manifestation and didn't take
Contemplation, no Persuasion.
"My Kinda Love is like no other."
Sincere and unbreakable, forgiving and unshakable.
Retraceable? DNA none listed
If ever to lose my Kinda Love.
Prepare for withdrawals, Heart and Mind, and Craving a Touch.
Again this Love DNA is none listed,
Search the love of many; I insist on it
Knowing it's my Love that must be revisited.

Equality

You came into my life and changed my world
To imagine life's journey without you will be a constant quarrel
Enjoy that we constantly learn, grow, and build
Sacred part of me holds truth and remains real deal
You showed that love can be reciprocated and pure,
Leaving no doubts and no guessing, assured and secure.
My request other than loyalty, is for you to love me
And be patient, while I offer the same in such a fashion,
Through the longest distance, Burn Passion.

G*Baybee

No matter the weather, the wetter the better
Your infinite treasure is indeed a pleasure
The pleasure of your sweet lips
Kisses that are above or below your sweet hips
Both which are magnificent gifts
Your sex appeal is beyond real, many can't deal
So, it's no surprise why you are queen in my eyes
With the style and grace that no woman can trace
As I trace the lines on my way
Only to display your majestic, loved, respected, and highly eclectic
And I'll down the first that disagrees with esoteric…

K. Antwon Buckner

A Love High That's Deep

You're the wind beneath my wings
The air that I breathe
Knowing endearment with loyalty cannot be quantified
The balance affirms it's complete
When nightfall arrives many count sheep
Though I count the you's to go to sleep
The uniqueness of love sustains one with peace
And the depths of that measures deep.

It's You

Who would have thought?
My anchor in this storm of life
Would help me navigate successfully
Towards the brightening lights
To be alone?
You're complete.
But like my goals,
I aim to reach
A point in life
Where you're my wife
So our dreams intertwine each day
Like sunshine...

More Than a Thought

More than an idea,
Know to be able to act,
Demonstrate by turning dreams, plots, plans, and thoughts
Into reality.
Conceive, believe, and achieve
At every chance,
Excelling on a level of greatness
Whether obtained already or in pursuit of.
We are the extraordinary.
Through experience and observation
Downfalls many times are a result of the lack of preparation.
Undisciplined or not being able to avoid ordinary more simplistic things and measures.
Point- One must know how to tap into both thought processes...

Purpose and Passion

When we believe in ourselves, our actions will support it.
When we find our purpose, success comes when we believe
our passion and purpose is greater than any opposition or challenge.
The reward and greatest peace is found in discovering
our purpose and achieving our passion.

K. Antwon Buckner

Special

To say I'm satisfied is an understatement.
You blow my mind in many ways and there's no rating it.
Love, loyalty and trust you define
Something many look for, yet can't find
You move me with no words and just one look.
I'm satisfied in full my dear
And to the future I look.
No woman can come close or compare and that's no bull.
Your value is priceless,
And, I'm satisfied in full.

First Tattoo

The never-ending pain
Black ink oozing out
Blood soaking into the wet rag
Man! How bad this hurt
I hope the creation
Resembles my dedication
Cause everyone said
Art is to be expressed
What better way to speak my mind
Then to sit for hours on end
No friend, just the person
Responsible for this throbbing feeling I feel
In my arm that's coursing to my hand
My mind is screaming if I only knew
The pleasure and pain I received
From my first taboo
My lover's name and first tattoo.

About the Author

K. Antwon Buckner is a man with a message on love, self-love and love for family, friends, partners, and spouses. Through his own personal journey, exploration, and pursuit for passion, he has come to learn some of the necessary components of successful relationships and healthy living.

A Love of Your Own is his first novel, but with writing in his fingertips, he does not plan to stop there! Now, that you have read and enjoyed this book, stay wide-eyed and alert for his next book: *Kindred Souls*.